RETURN TO SCALE
Alternatives to globalisation

nef is an independent think-and-do tank that inspires and demonstrates real economic well-being.

We aim to improve quality of life by promoting innovative solutions that challenge mainstream thinking on economic, environmental and social issues. We work in partnership and put people and the planet first.

 economics
real wealth
means well-being

Current priorities include international
debt, transforming markets, global
finance and local economic renewal

 environment
lifestyles must
become sustainable

Current priorities are climate change,
ecological debt and local sustainability

 society
communities need
power and influence

Current priorities include democracy,
time banks, well-being and public services

nef The New Economics Foundation is a registered charity founded in 1986 by the leaders of The Other Economic Summit (TOES), which forced issues such as international debt onto the agenda of the G7/G8 summit meetings. It has taken a lead in helping establish new coalitions and organisations, such as the Jubilee 2000 debt campaign; the Ethical Trading Initiative; the UK Social Investment Forum; and new ways to measure social and environmental well-being.

Return to Scale, overview by Andrew Simms,
policy director of the New Economics Foundation
Contributions from: Nick Robins, Perry Walker, Satish Kumar, James Marriot,
Vicki Hird, Sarah Burns, Andrew Simms, David Boyle, John Ziman, Jay Griffiths,
Ed Mayo

Edited by David Boyle and Molly Conisbee, with thanks to Petra Kjell.

ISBN 1-899407-69-3

Registered charity number 1055254
Printed and bound in Great Britain by Tandem Press
www.tandempress.com

new economics foundation
3 Jonathan Street
London SE11 5NH
United Kingdom

Telephone: +44 (0)20 7820 6300
Facsimile: +44 (0)20 7820 6301
E-mail: info@neweconomics.org
Website: www.neweconomics.org
Registered charity number 1055254

RETURN TO SCALE
Alternatives to globalisation

*30 years on – economics as if people
and the planet mattered*

Contents

Chapter 1

Return to scale

An elephant moves
into an ant hill, shocked
by its own havoc

Andrew Simms

Scale matters. A single painkiller can cure a headache, but swallow a whole bottle and it will kill you. Whatever we do, the scale of our action is critical to its effect. Cut down a few trees and you can call it woodland management – clear-fell a forest and an entire ecosystem is destroyed.

Whether something is beneficial or destructive can simply be a function of the scale at which it happens. A firework is fun; a cluster bomb is not.

One of the biggest changes in the modern world is precisely our ability to do things on a massive scale. There have always been wars, but the destructive power of contemporary weapons mocks the most ferocious inventions of earlier ages. It is a long way from the longbow to the obliterating power of the cruise missile.

Why dwell on these examples? Because these insights from different areas of our lives appear to be common sense. Why, then, when it comes to the organisation of the global economy does a completely different assumption apply? Why, when we talk about how we all do business is there an expectation that, sooner or later, we should do it in a global market place; that a successful firm is one that gets bigger and bigger, and takes over other firms?

This assumption is now so ubiquitous, and has permeated so deeply into our consciousness, that few voices even are raised when it is brought to bear on previously exempt areas of our lives like health and education. When former corporate big cheese Richard Sykes took over at London's Imperial College, one of his first moves was to push a merger with another of London's leading colleges. Why did he assume it would be a good idea?

Increasingly, also, the 'big bias' is backed by law. If a country is a member of the World Trade Organisation or the International Monetary Fund, it has effectively signed away the freedom to ask:

what scale of economic organisation, what size of market, is right for the different sectors of its economy?

By joining either institution, a country becomes committed to full integration into global markets for finance, goods and services, regardless of whether or not they are right for it. Global institutions have actually legislated against the freedom to question the appropriateness of economic scale.

Recent years provide plenty of evidence about why this is a problem. The liberalisation of capital flows has created the conditions for ever bigger and more damaging financial crashes. After Mexico, Russia, Asia, the hedge fund crises, and the current US bubble economy, even conservative commentators on newspapers like the *Financial Times* recognise the rising dynamic of instability.

Global commodity markets display another downside of unmanageable 'bigness'. Developing countries are often heavily dependent for their export income on just a handful of products such as coffee, cocoa, sugar and cotton. But over the last few decades, these countries received bad advice from people in places like the World Bank who should have known better. They were all told that exporting more of the same stuff was the secret of economic development. The problem was that demand for these kinds of goods was relatively stable and, as their supply increased, prices started to fall. And, as everybody did the same thing, they kept falling so that poor countries – hooked into global markets – were running faster to stand still. Over the course of a decade, Ghana increased its cocoa production by 80 per cent but its income went up just two per cent.

All commodities except fuel reduced in real terms by 50 per cent from 1980. Benin is dependent on cotton for 84 per cent of her exports. But cotton prices fell by 30 per cent over just two years ending up at less than half of their 1995 levels, and coffee prices in 2001 were less than half the levels they were in 1999 – devastating for countries like Ethiopia.

So scale matters.

Instability in the global environment is another consequence of our blindness to issues of scale. It is easy to stand up and defend the 'right' of everyone to own a car. But even before that right is extended beyond a wealthy global minority, the lucky few have bought into lifestyles whose dependence on fossil fuels is driving global warming which in turn denies the 'rights' of millions to live and work in homes and towns vulnerable to climate change.

Scale matters, quite simply, because it can be a matter of life and death.

So why has it been so comprehensively ignored, or its importance misunderstood by mainstream economics?

Open a typical dictionary of economics and, if mentioned at all, scale is discussed only in the sense that firms can gain 'economies' from scale. Or, in other words, they can make more money by being big. Money is the single arena in which a major debate on scale has occurred. Economists have argued exhaustively over what is the optimal geographical area for a currency to function well – the almost mystical 'optimal currency zone'. Ironically, one result of that debate is that Europe now has the euro to challenge the dollar. The world now has two big currencies instead of one.

But, as David Boyle points out, what we really need are currencies working at lots of levels from the town to the global, in order to create a dynamic and flexible monetary system capable of responding to complex and contradictory economic, environmental and social problems.

Yet outside the orthodox community of economists, and mostly on the margins of intellectual enquiry, the debate about appropriateness of scale has raged. And, some of its key concepts have emerged in unlikely places. E.F. Schumacher's book *Small is Beautiful* – a title which, incidentally, he is said to have disliked and which was forced on to him by his publisher Anthony Blond – is hailed as the classic analysis of scale and also as one of the founding texts of the green movement.

But Schumacher modestly defers to the Catholic Church as the authors of the notion of 'subsidiarity' – the idea that things are always best done at the lowest practicable level.

Pope Pius XII described the 'principle of subsidiary function' in this way:

> "It is an injustice and at the same time a grave evil and disturbance of right order to assign to a greater and higher association what lesser and subordinate organisations can do."

By observing this principle, the encyclical says, "the stronger will be the social authority and effectiveness and the happier and more prosperous the condition of the state".

Subsidiarity re-emerged in the early 1990s around Europe as the political pressure valve on the cooking pot of the single European project. Politicians could be seen struggling with the term on evening news programmes – not entirely certain of its meaning –

trying to either explain or condemn it. Bruised by the experience, the concept retreated to the offices of eurocrats and academics, only to resurface now, much later, as the anti-globalisation movement searches for the theoretical underpinnings of the different world order they seek.

But even before Schumacher's book came out, another economist, Leopold Kohr, wrote the definitive attack on what goes wrong when things get too big. *The Breakdown of Nations* was published in 1957, still in the shadow of the Second World War. Kohr wrote that he was searching for a single theory to describe human activities and social organisation. He saw his quest being as bold as the search by physicists for a single theory to explain the universe. And the conclusion he came to was unequivocal:

> "The result is a new and unified political philosophy centring in the theory of size. It suggests that there seems only one cause behind all forms of human misery: bigness.
> Oversimplified as this may seem, we shall find the idea more easily acceptable if we consider that bigness, or oversize, is really much more than just a social problem. It appears to be the one and only problem permeating all creation. Wherever something is wrong, something is too big...
> On a small scale, everything becomes flexible, healthy, manageable, and delightful, even a babies ferocious bite. On a large scale, on the other hand, everything becomes unstable and assumes the proportions of terror."

Today we could quibble with Kohr. We could say that things can also go wrong and can assume the 'proportions of terror' if they are also too small. Oppressive states can use minute surveillance technology to spy on its people. In the wrong hands, the fingerprint of your unique life code – your DNA – could be used against you, for example by insurance companies in predicting your susceptibility to illnesses and applying a kind of 'economic eugenics'.

Biotechnology and nanotechnology give us plenty of cause for concern, but again the problem is one of scale. These processes manipulate life and matter at a level so small that the consequences are hard to predict. Every field trial of a genetically engineered plant is, effectively, the full environmental release of a new life-form whose impact is difficult, if not impossible, to predict – what one car-bumper sticker called 'giving pollution a life of its own.'

There is growing concern also in the scientific community that

4

nanotechnology could also create products that are impossible to control, and could ultimately work against human kind. But again problems arise especially where these technologies are applied on a large scale, for example in commercial agriculture. Nature is perfectly capable of crossing genetic information between plants and animals and among plants, but it does so on occasional basis. It doesn't develop a new crop in a laboratory and then plant it abruptly in several million acres.

We now know it is not just about ideas of absolute size; it is about appropriateness. Schumacher's own words describe why the lens of scale is an under-used analytical tool:

> "There is wisdom in smallness if only on account of the smallness and patchiness of human knowledge, which relies on experiment far more than on understanding. The greatest danger invariably arises from the ruthless application, on a vast scale, of partial knowledge such as we are currently witnessing in the application of nuclear energy, of the new chemistry in agriculture, of transportation technology, and countless other things."

Little has changed in the 30 years since *Small is Beautiful* was published. Some issues have got much worse. In Schumacher's day, global warming – a consequence of the scale of our consumption of fossil fuels – had been predicted, but was far from a major concern. But conservation was, and future generations will almost certainly look back aghast at the reckless squandering in the past three decades of a earth's fossil inheritance that took millions of years to build-up.

It is a popular misconception that Schumacher thought everything should be small scale. Actually he thought that: "The burden of proof lies always on those who want to deprive a lower level of its function, and thereby of its freedom and responsibility... they have to prove that the lower level is incapable of fulfilling this function satisfactorily and that the higher level can actually do much better."

With no apparent sense of irony, Kirkpatrick Sale wrote a very large, heavy book of more than 550 pages and called it *Human Scale*. Published in 1980, it gathered together a huge body of evidence to show that things work better when they operate on a human scale. He looked at food production, waste disposal, the optimum size for convivial communities, transport, health, education, and architecture among other things. He also looked at energy, following Ivan Illich's earlier classic *Energy and Equity,* which itself is a classic treatise on the question of scale in relation to energy – how we produce it and how we consume it.

Since these landmark works were written, many have tried to put their principles into action. A contemporary of Schumacher's and a co-founder of the New Economics Foundation (NEF), George McRobie, wrote *Small is Possible.* Others such as Manfred Max-Neef tried to construct theoretical models for the application of human scale development. Countless individuals, often derided for dropping out of society, have tried to live their lives also according to the ideas.

Yet all the time that this work was going on, two contradictory things have happened. The writers and activists have been proved right, but things have continued to get bigger. In the process, they have also often gone wrong.

Democracy: Big remote electoral processes and the centralisation of power in Western democracies is killing the ballot box. People have voted, or rather not, with their feet. Turn-out rates on polling day have crashed hitting record lows in Britain and America. People are disillusioned with one of the great human triumphs of the last century – electoral democracy. It is now clear that to restore vitality and participation in the democratic process the opposite must happen. Communities need power and control over issues that affect them. People need to believe that there is a point to becoming active citizens.

Wealth: Several decades of globalisation have driven the gap between rich and poor ever wider. Measured by income, the picture is dramatic. Measured by assets, the gap is even bigger. This is not a failure of markets under a neo-liberal system, but the definition of their success. Increasingly unfettered markets have allowed wealth or capital to accumulate in the hands of a global elite – mostly in the North, but in the South too.

Food: Small farms have proven to be more productive than large farms. And international research programmes such as Biodepth have proven that more plant diversity means higher productivity. These simple insights fundamentally contradict the standard approach to commercial agriculture with its emphasis on big farms and factory style monoculture.

Corporations: Corporations keep getting bigger – in spite of the fact that over two thirds of mergers and acquisitions fail to bring business benefits. As they do, two things happen. Power concentrates in the economy and people lose their trust in business. There have always been large corporations, but a distinctly new phenomenon has emerged in recent years. In food retailing, banking, or professional services like the accountants, small operators are dying out and a growing market share is controlled by ever few companies. NEF set up a newsletter, MergerWatch, to monitor these trends.

Property: Globally land ownership continues to concentrate into ever fewer hands and intellectual property, protected by law, is largely held by a tiny global elite of corporations, governments and research institutes.

Economy: The proportion of economic activity taking place on the global stage, for example international trade in goods and services as a share of gross national product, has grown along with the massive growth over the last half a century of trading in foreign exchange – about $2 trillion a day now changes hands on the global markets.

But there is no point in growing more food if the way you do it exacerbates the conditions of poverty. And there is no point in generating more power if the way you do it destroys the atmosphere, and the conditions for life in the process.

One reason for the persistent failure of mainstream economics, even today, to address the question of scale is because the damages from 'bigness' – in terms of pollution, human alienation and social breakdown – fall outside the balance sheet. It is part of the equally persistent failure of economics to give proper value to the well-being of the wider system. And the failure of insight to understand that the economy is a 'wholly-owned subsidiary of the environment and human society'.

In the global economy, things just keep getting bigger, regardless of consequences. It is time for a return to scale. But how?

Behind you!

There is a typical moment in pantomime in which the principal character toys with the emotions of the audience. They might be searching for the love of a prince or princess, or trying to escape an evil predator. The lurking thing or person is always just out-of-view behind them. Then, in a camp and highly disingenuous manner, the principal character refuses to see what is behind them and keeps on looking. All the time goading the audience, which shouts in chorus: *"Behind you!"*

This scenario is played out time and again in the pantomime of economic globalisation. For at least the last two decades the faults in the system have been comprehensively exposed: debt crises, financial crashes, environmental degradation, corporate malpractice and a rigged international trading system that works against the interests of poor countries.

Yet there is always a character centre-stage who refuses to see the countless alternatives to business-as-usual. Economist or newspaper editor, government minister or mandarin of an international financial institution: they are always on stage looking to the left and right unable to see what is right behind them. We in the audience scream our heads off – behind you! – the answer is *behind you*. And they stand there, hand cupped to their ear, pretending to want to hear us, and pretending not to hear us.

But the time has come for the curtain to fall on this cheap theatre. Economic globalisation is walking hand-in-hand with a rise in global instability: environmental, financial and political. People are suffering and dying as a result.

This collection is an extended invitation to look again at the issue of scale, as we search for answers to the problems of globalisation. It was for this reason that NEF organised a series of events called *Return to Scale* at the London-based *Institute of Contemporary Arts*. They have systematically explored areas as diverse as technology, money, energy, consumerism and trade using the analytical tool of the lens of scale. These chapters have either come from, or been inspired by these events. They show how it is possible to see the world and organise our affairs in completely different ways.

They demonstrate that one of the most important questions we can ask is: what is the right scale for this to work best? Or, at what level do we maximise the economic, social and environmental benefits of what we do, and minimise the costs?

If local is the best level to do something, it will be different depending on what that thing is. For example, baking bread, growing food or building trains.

Since NEF began again to focus on the issue of scale, the meaning of 'local' has changed. An old Chinese proverb – why *are* they always Chinese? – goes that when two elephants meet, whether they fight or make love, the consequence for the grass beneath their feet is the same.

So it is with the merged corporate giants of the modern global economy. Multinational brewing group Interbrew sued multinational bank HSBC in the Netherlands, France and Belgium for its use of the phrase 'The world's local bank'. Interbrew uses the phrase 'The world's local brewer' in its marketing and claimed intellectual copywright to the words 'The world's local...'

What has happened to the idea of the local? Once oppressive and inward, local was for too long synonymous with neighbourhood net curtain-twitching, and was the last refuge of those terrified by the modern world.

Suddenly it has become the definition of truly modern. Local is to economics what organic has become to food: healthy, real and connected. Multinationals are prepared to go to court to defend their 'local' credentials.

What is going on? Several years of anti-globalisation protests may not have created checks and balances on corporations at the global level. But they have fed deep suspicions that big business has little interest in public well-being. NEF's report *What's Trust Worth?* showed a steady decline in the number of people who think 'most companies are fair to consumers'. So, business is polishing its public relations to deal with the alienation that has grown out of its bigness, fat-cattery and ruthless ambition.

In a use of language that would add nicely to George Orwell's 1984 list of doublethink, the bigger a company gets, the more oblique and distant its real ownership becomes, and the more it swallows up countless smaller firms, the more it is likely to claim to be local.

NEF revealed in the report *Ghost Town Britain* that the costs of consolidation in numerous economic sectors were killing local economies. As banks like HSBC got bigger and bigger, over a quarter of Britain's bank branch network was lost between 1990-2000. And, as they fight with Interbrew, the same trend is even visible in our brewing trade. Just three breweries now produce about 80 per cent of Britain's beer. Country pubs are closing at the rate of nearly one a day and over 130 regional and national brands of beer have been lost since 1990.

A new cultural movement is slowly emerging in favour of alternatives to the miserable banality and alienation of corporate and finance driven globalisation. It is visible in the spread of slow food and slow city campaigns. You can smell it in the growing number of

What are the ingredients?

Localisation	vs	Globalisation
Distinctiveness		Uniformity
Nearness		Distance
Diversity		Homogeneity
Markets as a means to an end		Markets as their own end
Profits stay local		Profits go to remote shareholders
Benefits go to economically/ socially active people		Benefits go to owners of finance
Rules to manage abuse of power		Deregulation
Social cohesion a particular objective		Social cohesion not considered
Subsidiarity		Any level dictated by market actors
Optimising economic activity		Maximising economic activity
Something you do yourself		Something that is done to you

farmers markets, and hear the bustle of activity coming out of time banks across Britain. It even has its own political edge in the NEF-supported *Local Communities and Sustainability Bill*.

Ghost Town Britain argued that diverse and dynamic local economies create the glue which holds communities together. But at the same time, big, remote businesses like the supermarkets get supported disproportionately through a range of tax breaks, absence of competition rules and planning support. They get this support because successive governments have swallowed the lie that they are more efficient and competitive.

Yet enjoying near monopoly status, they do not operate in a meaningfully competitive market. Where the big four might control up to a quarter of the retail food market nationally, in a given local area their monopoly control may be almost total. Nor are they efficient: employing fewer people for every pound of turnover compared to smaller, truly local stores, they cause a net loss of retail jobs and do not sell the 'glue' that holds communities together.

Even in this already highly concentrated market, consolidation is creeping forward. At the time of writing the major British supermarkets including Tesco, Sainsbury, Asda/Walmart and smaller chain Morrisons are hovering over the Safeway chain, the subject of multiple moves to take-over its business.

There is a cultural as well as economic irony here. The state centralist economies of old Central and Eastern Europe were once derided for the grey uniformity of their urban environments. When these states collapsed, the West's business community crowed in triumph. But today, on our doorsteps, a kind of 'corporate centralism' is bringing its own bland, indistinguishable monotony to the streets of our towns and cities.

A particularly cruel animal experiment explains why big business also needs saving from itself. Researchers found that frogs placed in water that heats up very slowly lacked the physiological ability to tell when the temperature became dangerously warm, allowing themselves to be cooked to death. Likewise, as concentration in multiple economic sectors increases, corporations lack the feedback mechanisms to warn that things are going wrong until it is too late.

A spate of failures from energy giant Enron to communications giant WorldCom and professional services firm Andersen stand like dead warning carcasses along the road of corporate hubris. The careers and savings of thousands were left in the wreckage. But even below the radar of these spectacular failures, things are not good. Research by equally large accountancy firm KPMG showed that less than a third of corporate mergers and acquisitions actually added value. In a 1999 survey over half were shown to destroy value, falling to a third in the economically more cautious new millennium.

So much for the bad news. If the visionaries of decades ago failed to turn their ideas into reality, why should it be any different now?

First, even big business needs a well and stable society in which to operate. The many levels of insecurity and instability, economic, political, environmental and social, that are emerging are bad for business. Any residual faith in 'rational economic people' suggests that the light should come on sooner or later.

But there is another, more compelling reason. Real change follows major social movements. The big campaigns of the last half of the last century were for civil rights, the welfare state, sexual equality and peace.

Today's political context is dominated by the impact of corporate and finance-led globalisation. The big new social movement is an international force calling for an alternative. This movement is wildly eclectic. In forming its response to economic globalisation it needs organising principles. Doing things at the lowest practicable scale –

subsidiarity – is one of them. It means that international bodies and agreements are needed to manage and arbitrate business that goes on globally, but also that local communities should have the power to decide their own local development path.

Localisation is also the obvious antithesis of globalisation. There is a simple, strong logic to rallying to it. The story localisation tells is the opposite to one in which remote profits accumulate for a tiny minority, where all our shopping streets look the same, and there are ever-widening gaps between rich and poor.

Critics of the dark side of globalisation have alternatives to offer – hundreds of them. This collection gives a flavour. The year 2003 is the 30th anniversary of the publication of *Small is Beautiful*, what Schumacher called 'a study of economics as if people mattered.' It offered a new paradigm for a struggling discipline. Given the fragile state of the global economy and environment, what at first sounded like merely a desirable good idea, has become for many a matter of life and death.

Andrew Simms is policy director of the New Economics Foundation.

September 2003

NB. The reader will notice that each chapter begins with a short haiku-like poem. In the spirit of this book, and the events at the ICA that they mostly came from, they are an attempt at the ultimate in executive summary.

Chapter 2

Corporations

Tall rock, the firm
towers above us until
water wears it down

Downsizing the corporation and the need for open markets
Nick Robins

The rise of corporate concentration is now a central feature of today's global economy. It is now a commonplace that 51 of the world's largest economies are corporations[i]. Globalisation, privatisation and deregulation have all led to a surge in both corporate conglomeration and market sharing cartels. But thriving economies depend on open competition and restrictions of corporate size to prevent abuse of market power. It is therefore no surprise that the question of corporate scale is increasingly being targeted as a problem in its own right[ii].

Box 1: Transforming the Corporation –
The Seven Axes of Change[iii]

There are seven linked but logically independent elements to transforming the modern corporation so that it better serves the public interest.

1. **Scale:** Globalisation, privatisation and deregulation have all led to a surge in both corporate conglomeration and market sharing cartels. But thriving economies depend on open competition and restrictions of corporate size to prevent abuse of market power.

2. **Practices:** This is the starting point for most reform efforts – pressing companies through law or voluntary effort, to improve their operations, through business ethics policies, workplace programmes, and environmental initiatives.

3. **Transparency:** Closely linked to the task of getting improved practices is the urgency of making sure that corporations disclose their performance and are publicly accountable for their actions – a priority if the marketplace is to fully internalise corporate costs and benefits.

4. **Technology:** In some cases, the problems at stake with key corporations are intrinsic to the technology they use, requiring actions to

---

13

phase-out their use - like nuclear power or tobacco. Genetic modification has also exposed the problem of corporate control over the research process, and the need to insert the precautionary principle and public oversight into the heart of technological innovation.

5. **Governance**: The right to decide is crucial for any institution, and in most cases, executive power in corporations rests exclusively with management. Measures to introduce worker involvement in the wake of the Second World War, such as Germany's co-determination structures, offer working models of corporate governance that offer key stakeholders, such as workers, a share in decision-making.

6. **Ownership**: The corporation has become synonymous with private ownership. But the excesses of shareholder-controlled companies - combined with the negative experience of privatisation in many countries - has revealed the need for more diverse patterns of corporate ownership, embracing the new mutualism and wider employee ownership.

7. **Purpose**: The single-minded focus of the modern corporation on profit maximisation for shareholders conveys an impoverished vision of corporate purpose. Company law needs to be rewired so that corporate goals match the complexity of the environment in which they operate.

Indeed, ever since the emergence of the corporation in the late 18th century, the issue of scale has been a continuous concern. At its heart, Adam Smith's *Wealth of Nations* is a critique of the prevailing mercantilist belief in monopolies, such as the East India Company, and a call for open market competition based on small-scale production.

But the removal of these traditional statutory monopolies soon gave way to the emergence of new 'manufactured monopolies' in the Victorian Age. The struggle against these trusts – combining the defence of the public interest with the promotion of the principle of open markets – defined half a century of American economic history from the 1870s, leading to the break-up of Standard Oil and the tobacco trusts just prior to the First World War. The crash of 1929 prompted further measures to break-up the financial establishment, notably the 1933 Glass-Steagall Act to separate commercial and investment banking.

Ultimately, however, legal restraints served only to stem the worst excesses, and failed to "have much bearing on the concentration of economic activity"[iv]. While market dominance by a few key firms (oligopoly) breached the tenets of neo-classical theory, it was increasingly accepted in practice across the world. As John Kenneth Galbraith concluded in the 1970s, "King Canute looks down on those who administer our antitrust laws with the utmost understanding and sympathy"[v].

Since then, 30 years of privatisation, deregulation and trade liberalisation have undone many of these modest gains, and created new global combinations to replace the national 'champions' of an earlier age. The result is a crisis of control that demands a similarly robust approach to global anti-trust as inspired reformers in the last century. Not only is such a global anti-trust approach economically urgent, but it also offers the prospect of a powerful new alliance between those supporting open markets and those aiming to curb corporate power.

For if there is to be real progress towards a more accountable, just and sustainable global economy, then a fundamental shift of economic metaphor is required. This means abandoning the unrealistic notion of the 'free market'. In a situation where the world's top 500 corporations control 70 per cent of international commerce, it is becoming increasingly misleading to talk of 'free trade'. Instead, the focus should shift towards the promotion of 'open markets', where – like Popper's Open Society – diversity is stimulated through an active competition policy, transparency is ensured through comprehensive disclosure and choice is based on prices that reflect full social and environmental costs.

But before turning to how 21st century anti-trust could best be achieved at the local, national and global levels, it is worth reminding ourselves why corporate concentration has become such a problem for the effective functioning of the market and the wider public good.

The seven sins of corporate concentration

Economic theory teaches us that markets work best when competition is generated through the interaction of a multiplicity of buyers and sellers, and when no one player is big enough to skew prices and conditions in their direction. Yet, although competition is essential for the effective working of the market economy, it is not a natural phenomenon, and needs to be nurtured and often forced into existence through regulation and public oversight.

What is troubling, however, is that this idealised vision of the self-regulating market continues to inform the largely hands-off approach to competition and anti-trust policy. Neo-classical economics still only has one theory of the firm, and cannot distinguish between a one-man barber and a multinational corporation. This stance is generally defended on the basis of the benefits that are deemed to flow from economies of scale – particularly in international and technologically complex conditions – and from a defeatism that points to the need for companies to grow if they are to compete against other global giants.

The rapid pace of globalisation has brought this often wilfully naïve faith into question. A series of recent competition enquiries have highlighted the tendency of market abuse from over-mighty corporations. Without an assertive competition policy in place, the potential benefits of privatisation, deregulation and trade liberalisation will be lost as companies merge to dominate markets and thereby remove the threat of competition to their profits.

The conclusions of a new study of the European power generation sector, for example, carried out by the Oko-Institut for the European Parliament, are illustrative of the wider trend. Years of privatisation and liberalisation have resulted in a situation where "market concentration in the field of power generation has to be seen as endangering fair, competitive and sustainable energy markets"[vi].

Falling barriers to trade have also stimulated a surge in cross-border mergers and acquisitions – peaking at just under $900 billion in 2000 – as firms consolidate to protect themselves from competition and dominate markets. Repeated crises in international financial markets have further accelerated this process of concentration: falling exchange rates and collapsing markets during the 1997 Asian crisis prompted a fire-sale of local firms to international companies at knock-down prices. Taken together, this dash for scale has many negative consequences for other market participants and the wider public good, which can be summarised as the 'seven sins of corporate concentration'.

Increased prices: Basic economics teaches that reduced supply will generate increased prices, and so it proves time and again. According to Consumers International, unregulated globalisation is leading to an "explosive growth of global price fixing and market sharing cartels", with the result that "each day consumers are being robbed of millions of dollars"[vii]. At a national level in the UK, the inflationary impacts of concentration are best seen in the banking sector. Here, the largest four banks – Barclays, HSBC, LloydsTSB and the Royal Bank of Scotland – control two-thirds of the market for individual current accounts and over 90 per cent of services to small and medium sized enterprises. A recent Competition Commission enquiry identified a number of specific practices that restrict and/or distort price competition in the SME market, resulting in excessive profits for the four banks of about £725 million a year[viii].

Abuse of market power: It is not just consumers whose rights are abused through corporate concentration. Suppliers to companies that dominate the marketplace also find their terms and conditions squeezed. The food processing and retail sectors exemplify the forces at work. Key global commodity chains have become highly concentrated, generating powerful downward pressure on the prices of goods exported by many developing countries. In the cocoa trade, for example, over 40 per cent of processing is controlled by just four firms, while three-quarters of chocolate sales in Europe are accounted for by three companies (Cadbury, Nestle and Mars)[ix], hampering the functioning of the market to the disadvantage of cocoa producing nations. But the problem is not confined to international markets. Diversity in food retail at the national level has been steadily shrunk as the large supermarket chains acquire their rivals and drive others out of business. In the USA, the top five retailers controlled 42 per cent of food sales in 2000, up from 24 per cent only three years earlier[x], while in France, the top five controlled 83 per cent of food sales in 2001, up from 53 per cent just five years earlier[xi]. In Britain, the top five supermarkets account for 80 per cent of food sales – "a complex monopoly situation", according to the Competition Commission. The Commission also found "a climate of apprehension" existing among supermarket suppliers, who faced over 50 predatory practices from their supermarket clients, including requiring non-cost discounts, making changes to contracts without notice and unreasonably transferring risks to the supplier[xii]. And as one part of the value chain comes together, so suppliers are forced to consolidate and cut costs – often with serious social consequences, as the redundancies announced by Danone in 2001 exemplified.

Biased innovation: Corporate concentration is also a powerful force for steering technological innovation – often in ways that go against the public interest. The long-standing competition case against Microsoft in the USA and Europe highlights just how quickly new monopolies can be generated in areas of rapid technological change – blocking new entrants and generating excess profits from dominant positions. The spread of renewable energy in the power sector could also become constrained by the dominance of a few key players. But it is perhaps in the 'life science' business where concentration is having the most perverse effect on the trajectory of technological development. The sector is dominated by seven 'gene giants' (Syngenta, Pharmacia, Aventis, BASF, Dupont, Bayer and Dow) that straddle the biotechnology, agrochemical, seeds and pharmaceutical sectors[xiii]. The result is a capital-intensive model of proprietary genetic engineering, pushed ahead without sufficient regard to potential impacts on human health, farming livelihoods or the environment in order that shareholder returns can be earned as quickly as possible.

Reduced diversity: Strong links exist between open markets and social diversity. Not surprisingly, corporate concentration can often bring uniformity – a particularly troubling phenomenon in the global media sector, where seven players now own virtually all aspects of the media experience (AOL TimeWarner, Newscorp, Disney, Viacom, Vivendi, Bertelsman and Sony). Speaking on World Press Freedom Day 2002, Czech president Vaclav Havel declared that "fifty years from now, the globalisation process may be the biggest threat to freedom of expression"[xiv]. Sadly, media regulation appears to be buckling under the pressure from these global giants, with Britain's new Communications Bill opening up some of the last restricted areas to consolidation and foreign takeover: "it's open season", commented one City banker, anticipating a surge in mergers and acquisitions[xv].

Unequal benefits: The growing size of corporations also skews the distribution of benefits between employees, management and shareholders. According to KPMG, 70 per cent of mergers and acquisitions fail to achieve their objectives or raise shareholder value; of these 39 per cent actually lead to lower returns for investors[xvi]. Employees also lose out, as jobs are often cut following mergers: 130,000 jobs were lost in Europe's finance sector alone during the 1990s. If investors and employees are losing out, the real beneficiaries of growing concentration are clearly company managers, along with the range of legal and financial advisers who earn fees from M&A activity. Managers of larger firms get paid more, with mergers leading to a doubling of executive pay, according to a Royal

Economic Society study[xvii]. The current passivity of competition policy in the face of the welfare destroying impacts of concentration is thus indirectly fortifying the position of corporate executives at the expense of other key stakeholders.

Political manipulation: As institutions, corporations are not simply economic actors, and increased scale gives firms greater scope for manipulating both the political process and regulatory framework in their favour. While much lobbying is done through industry associations, the most effective leverage is engaged by big firms operating on their own account: pushing for changes to the law, pressing for tax reductions and new subsidies, and influencing the planning process. Bigness gives companies the ability to not only reduce their contribution to the public good – and thereby shifting the burden of taxation onto individuals – but also skew public spending priorities onto areas of immediate interest (corporate welfare). Concentration at the global level further magnifies these longstanding problems by placing transnational corporations in a position both to weaken the negotiating position of governments, and thus, undermine national sovereignty, while at the same time enjoying privileged status in key global decision-making institutions, such as the World Trade Organisation.

Conflicts of interest: As companies grow, so their activities can straddle functions that need to be kept separate to keep markets open. The Enron scandal helped to expose the growing conflict of interest between the auditing and consultancy arms of the big accountancy firms, while the implosion of the dot.com bubble revealed the dubious practices of many investment banks, within only fragile 'Chinese walls' dividing stock broking analysts and investment banking. To date, these issues have been addressed through voluntary restraints. But these are unlikely to eradicate the problem, which will ultimately require "breaking down the behemoths that financial deregulation has created"[xviii].

Corporate concentration not only violates the principles of effective open markets, but also leads to a substantial transfer of power and financial resources from consumers, taxpayers and small enterprises towards a narrow business elite. Although the tendency to concentration is inherent in deregulated markets, a key factor that drove the surge in mergers and acquisitions in the 1990s was the linking of executive remuneration to size rather than performance. This gave executives perverse incentives for ill-thought through conglomerations that rarely delivered financial returns, let alone benefits for workers, the community or the environment.

Concentration also denies choice to consumers, employees and investors, and thus frustrates the rising desire of these groups to express their social values through the marketplace. To reverse this tendency, a new regulatory framework is needed that moves from simply managing the process of inevitable consolidation, and seeks once again to bust the trusts.

21st century anti-trust

The damage done by corporate concentration is now increasingly recognised. But few have focused on the obvious next step of taking active measures to first halt and then turn back the tide. Even Schumacher's *Small is Beautiful,* with its passionate critique of the "idolatry of gigantism", makes no proposals for real reform[xix].

Today, however, the time for creative thinking to tackle the problems of scale is ripe. The excesses of the 1990s have exposed the multiple dangers of deregulated commerce. Competition authorities in the USA and Europe have started to become notably more assertive in recent years – highlighted by the Microsoft case, and the banking and retail enquiries in the UK. Discussion of the need and possible structure of a global competition regime has also burgeoned – with the EU in particular pressing for the World Trade Organisation to extend its remit to competition in the current Doha round of trade talks[xx].

In this context, seven priorities emerge for action to turn the tide:

De-link executive remuneration from corporate scale: As part of the wider reform of corporate governance that is needed following the string of corporate scandals in Europe and America, executive remuneration needs to be reformulated not only to bring it more in line with overall pay packages, but also to remove any incentive for managers to engage in takeovers simply to boost their own pay. If executives are to be rewarded with special bonuses then these need to be linked to performance across a range of criteria, including long-term returns to shareholders, employee well-being, community benefit and environmental stewardship.

Break-up conglomerations with conflicts of interest: Investment banks and accountancy firms have become key players in the new global economy. Their influence is not just connected to their size – and welcome moves are being considered to review the competitive effects of concentration in the audit sector – but also to the fact that they straddle different sub-sectors, giving them superior commercial advantages. Internal 'Chinese walls' have proved to be inadequate to prevent the emergence of conflicts of interest, and the formal separation of audit and consulting, banking and broking into independent firms needs to take place.

Introduce the standstill principle: In the wider economy, an initial step could be made by reversing the current burden of proof in favour of scale by introducing the standstill principle into competition policy – taking the position that no further growth in corporate scale should occur in key sectors of the economy. This would send a clear signal to both companies and investors that future growth could no longer have to take place through market dominating acquisitions.

Apply the roll-back principle: Stopping things getting worse is clearly the first priority – one that can be further developed by applying the roll-back principle in sectors where concentration is damaging the public interest. New enquiries need to be launched at the national and regional levels in key sectors – such as banking, food retail, life sciences, oil and power generation – not only to assess the scale of concentration, but also to design strategies for promoting corporate diversity and innovation, and the results phased-in over the next decade.

Require a public interest assessment of all new mergers and acquisitions: Scale is not always a problem, and can bring benefits to society. But at present, companies wanting to merge with and acquire others – implicitly reducing competition – are not required to demonstrate these supposed gains, or justify the likely costs to workers, shareholders and the wider community. To tackle this gap in corporate accountability, all mergers and acquisitions should be assessed for their wider public impacts by the competition authorities in a fully consultative process.

Launch global anti-trust investigations: Discussions about a global competition regime have been hampered so far by linking the debate to the future of the World Trade Organisation. It is entirely inappropriate to extend the mandate of the WTO further away from its core focus, particularly into an area of such sensitivity. Efforts should rather be placed on launching targeted global anti-trust investigations in areas of critical concern for the developing world – such as corporate concentration in key commodity sectors. These enquiries could be managed by specially constituted task forces, bringing together experts from leading competition authorities, and chaired on a provisional basis by UNCTAD. Remedies – including corporate restructuring – would still only be able to be demanded by national authorities, but the demonstration effect would be powerful. The results of these would most likely highlight the need for a more formal and independent global competition authority.

Target local monopolies: As globalisation has progressed, so the relevant market that the competition authorities assess for monopoly has expanded from the national to the regional and the global. Yet some of the most damaging effects can be felt at the local level – for example, with supermarkets able to gain a stranglehold over a community, even though their market-share nationally does not breach the current 25 per cent threshold. Local authorities and trading standards officers need to be empowered to continually test market conditions, and where necessary, force companies to give up market share to promote local development.

The extent of corporate concentration is now damaging markets, reducing choice and harming the public interest. A new and more assertive anti-trust policy suited to the conditions of the 21st century is therefore essential if global markets are to serve consumers and society at large. Downsizing the corporation will not only ensure greater economic diversity, but will also help create a more open and, thereby, sustainable global market.

Nick Robins, is head of research on socially responsible investment at Henderson Global Investors and writes in a personal capacity. He would like to thand Bill Vorley for his assistance in identifying data on concentration in agricultural markets.

i   It is less well known that this is not a new phenomenon: in 1969, 54 of the world's top economies were corporations. See Charles Levinson, *Capital, Inflation and the Multinationals*, George Allen & Unwin, London, 1971, p.104
ii   One sign of the times was the recent decision taken by the well-respected Canadian NGO, the Rural Advancement Foundation International, to change its name to the Action Group on Erosion,

Technology and Concentration in order to highlight its focus on corporate power.

iii   See Nick Robins, *Profit in Need? Business, Sustainable Development and the Great Transformation* in Nigel Cross (ed), Evidence for Hope, Earthscan, forthcoming, 2002

iv   John Kenneth Galbraith, *A History of Economics*, Hamish Hamilton, London, 1987, p.163

v   John Kenneth Galbraith and Nicole Salinger, *Almost Everyone's Guide to Economics*, Penguin, Harmondsworth, 1981, p.53

vi   Oko-Institut e.V., *Power Generation Market Concentration in Europe 1996-2000. An empirical analysis*, Freiburg, May 2002, www.oeko.de

vii   Consumers International, The Global Cartels Campaign – Fact Sheet, London, 2001

viii   Competition Commission, The supply of banking services by clearing banks to small and medium-sized enterprises – Summary, London, 2002

ix   Nick Robins & Sarah Roberts (ed), *The reality of sustainable trade*, IIED, London, April 2000

x   Public Citizen, *Down on the Farm: NAFTA's Seven-Years War on Farmers and Ranchers in the US and Mexico*, Washington, D.C., 2001

xi   Danone, *Corporate Social Responsibility Report 2001*, Paris, 2001

xii   Competition Commission, *Supermarket: A report on the supply of groceries from multiple stores in the United Kingdom*, London, 2000.

xiii   ETC Group, *Globalization, Inc. – Concentration in Corporate Power: The Unmentioned Agenda*, Issue # 71, July/August 2001

xiv   Quoted in Ian Hargreaves, The threat to democracy, *Financial Times*, 21 May 2002

xv   Quoted in James Harding & Ashling O'Connor, All set for merger and takeover frenzy, *Financial Times*, May 8, 2002

xvi   Quoted in *Mergerwatch*, Edition 2, New Economics Foundation, July 2001

xvii   Quoted in *Mergerwatch* – Edition 4, New Economics Foundation, October 2002

xviii   C.P. Chandrasekhar, The myth of market self-governance, *Frontline*, May 24 2002.

xix   E F Schumacher, *Small is Beautiful*, Blond & Briggs, London, 1973

xx   See CUTS Briefing Papers No4 *Competition Policy in a Globalising and Liberalising World Economy* (May 1996) & No8 *Globalisation: Enhancing Competition or Creating Monopolies* (2000) for useful overviews of the issues at stake.

Chapter 3

Democracy

Follow me, follow
me, he said, then asked
So, where shall we go?

From deliberation to democs
Perry Walker

In ancient Greece, democracy directly involved large numbers of those eligible, the free men. Public officials were chosen by lot from among the citizens. A quarter of free male adults served as president of Greece for 24 hours. This system has been held up as an ideal throughout history, but was condemned as unworkable for the size-able nation states that developed in Europe from the Renaissance onwards.

Democracy became feasible again when it was linked with the idea of representation. This had, in its origins, nothing to do with democracy: Edward I summoned a parliament because he needed agreement to taxation. But when it was added to the more direct Greek notion of democracy, representation became the answer to the problem of scale. An 18th century Frenchman described it as "democracy rendered practicable over a great extent of territory". In 1822, John Stuart Mill called it "the grand discovery of modern times".

Over time, the flaws in this grand discovery have appeared, as they do with any novelty. I will concentrate on three. First, the problem of scale re-emerged. The average constituency is over ten times the size it was in 1790. Not surprisingly, our representatives find it difficult to represent us. This is exacerbated by the culture that all elites develop, which further distances them from the people.

All this has reduced the legitimacy of representative government. In Europe, membership of political parties has fallen by nearly 50 per cent over the last 15 years. In 1998, turnout at local elections in England was 29 per cent, down from 45 per cent four years previ-ously. Nearly 70 per cent of young people in the UK have no interest in local politics.

People feel alienated. They are forever subjected to others' designs and reduced to data in others' programmes. They rarely feel themselves the authors of their own lives. According to John Routledge of Urban Forum: "Politics is the art of preventing people from taking part in affairs that concern them".

If distance and alienation make up the first flaw in our system, the second is that we have polarised debate rather than constructive dialogue. To explain this, I cannot do better than quote from an article from members of the Public Conversations Project, based in Massachusetts, USA:

> "Some controversies become defined by opposing views that cluster around two seemingly irreconcilable poles. A line [is drawn] between two simple answers to a complex dilemma and induces people to take a stand on one side of that line or the other. (For example, you are either a royalist or a revolutionary.) Most people who care deeply about the issue yield to this induction.

> Being aligned with one group offers benefits. It gives people a socially validated place to stand while speaking and it offers the unswerving support of like-minded people. It also exacts costs. It portrays opponents as a single-minded and malevolent gang. In the face of such frightening and unified adversaries, one's own group must be unified, strong, and certain. To be loyal to that group, one must suppress many uncertainties, morally complicated personal experiences, inner value conflicts, and differences between oneself and one's allies.

> Complexity and authenticity are sacrificed to the demands of presenting a unified front to the opponent. A dominant discourse of antagonism is self-perpetuating. Win-lose exchanges create losers who feel they must retaliate to regain lost respect, integrity, and security, and winners who fear to lose disputed territory won at great cost."

The third flaw in our system of representative government is a consequence of the first two. We, the people, are so far from the political system that we do not get the opportunities to form our opinions properly. The consequence of this is that our representatives represent not our opinions but our interests.

This seems strange, in the era of opinion polls. It was as long ago as 1888 that James Bryce MP described America as "Government by

Public Opinion". This was taken a stage further in 1936, when George Gallup forecast that Roosevelt would become president on the basis of a representative sample of a few thousand people. The *Literary Digest* scorned him beforehand, predicting a win for Alf Landon on the basis of millions of responses – which were unrepresentative.

But the value of such polls depends on the value of the opinions. The Theory of Rational Ignorance says that when any individual has so little influence, it is rational not to spend time learning about an issue and forming views upon it. In these circumstances, opinion polls can be undermined by the passivity that stems from alienation.

In the 1994 US election, there was an overheated debate on healthcare reform. Opinion polls showed widespread support for conflicting goals, summarised as: "One, lower my premiums, two, cover the uninsured, and lastly, solve the nation's cost problem". When confronted with details about how the uninsured were to be covered or how costs were to be contained, the support for these options changed markedly.

Hannah Arendt summarised this trenchantly: "Opinions are formed in a process of open discussion and public debate, and where no opportunity for the forming of opinion exists, there may be moods – moods of the masses and moods of individuals, the latter no less fickle and unreliable than the former – but no opinion".

Why we need active democracy

The privatisation of happiness: A recent BBC series, The Century of the Self, explored the legacy of Freud. It explained how the American radicals of the 1960s and 70s found the state a tougher nut to crack than they had expected. So they turned from taking on external authority to tackling internalised repression, 'the cop in the head'. From this came the fashion for EST, Encounter Groups and the like. But with a shift in means came a shift in ends. These radicals came to believe that to be happy they needed only to sort themselves out. They did not need to deal with the state. At times it appeared as if they did not need to deal with other people either. The legacy of this evolution is seen all over the western world, especially in advertising.

Public happiness: This attitude would have seemed bizarre throughout most of history. Partly this reflects a sense of duty. Pericles, the

26

Athenian orator, said: "We do not say that a man who takes no interest in politics is a man who minds his own business: we say that he has no business here at all." Mainly, though, this reflects a different sense of what it is to be human and what it is to be happy.

Benjamin Barber endorses Pericles in his book, *Strong Democracy.* "Human freedom", he says, "will be found not in caverns of private solitude but in the noisy assemblies where women and men meet daily as citizens and discover in each other's talk the consolation of a common humanity." Many would see this as a bit strong. Freedom means freedom to be private as well as to be public. But to live a purely private life is to tip the balance the other way.

The great sociologist Durkheim pointed out other benefits. He stated that in a cohesive society with high participation: "There is a constant interchange of ideas and feelings from all to each and each to all, something like a mutual moral support, which instead of throwing the individual on his own resources, leads him to share in the collective energy and supports his own when exhausted."

The evidence for the value of participation

The most striking statistical evidence comes from Switzerland. Two academics, Bruno Frey and Alois Stutzer, classified all the cantons on a six-point scale according to how participative they were. For example, the cantons vary in the number of signatures needed to launch a referendum. They then asked 6,000 Swiss residents how satisfied they were with their lives.

They found that a one-point increase in their participation scale increased the proportion of those who said they were very happy by 2.7 per cent. This is nearly half as big as the effect of moving from the lowest income band (around £11,000 a year) to the highest (£80,000 and upwards).

Frey and Stutzer were able to test whether greater happiness from higher participation was due to the outcome (better government) or to the process. Foreigners resident in Switzerland enjoy the outcomes, but are not allowed to take part in the process. Their happiness due to better government rose by only one-third as much as the increase for Swiss nationals. This implies that two-thirds of the benefits lie in the process, in the act of participation.

More anecdotal evidence on how participation widens people's horizons comes from the new deliberative methods described in the next chapter. People who have taken part in several of the US

National Issues Forums say that they start listening to the news more and in a different way, looking for options and their consequences. They also become more involved in civic activities – deliberation seems to get people to take the first step to civic involvement. Most participants (96 percent) with the Choices method, also described below, said that as a result they would look for similar discussions, to read more or to be more involved in civic affairs.

James Fishkin, inventor of the deliberative poll, was at the first one ever held, in Manchester in 1994. "A woman came up to me and said that during 30 years of marriage, her husband had never read a newspaper but that from the moment he had been invited to this weekend, he had changed. Not only did he read every bit of our briefing materials, but he now read 'every newspaper every day'. She speculated that he would be much more interesting to live with in retirement."

People also become more tolerant. In one deliberative poll: "At the beginning of one small group discussion on the family, an 84-year-old conservative from Arizona expressed the view that 'a family' required that there be both a mother and a father in the home. He spent three days in dialogue as part of a group that included a 41-year-old woman who had raised two children as a single parent. At the end of the weekend he went up to her and asked what three words in the English language 'can define a person's character'. He answered his own question with the words 'I was wrong'."

There is a visible reduction in stereotyping when different types of people come together in a setting where it is safe to explore their differences. Future Search conferences bring around 64 people together over two or three days. One event, called 'Youth Matters', took place in Forres in Aberdeenshire. Each event has a session called 'Prouds and Sorries' in which each stakeholder group to share their feelings. In Forres the 'sorries' included: 'Lack of communication' (Youth group), 'Not listening enough' (Community Organisations Group), and 'Although listening more, ignoring most of what is heard' (Authority group). It is very powerful to be able to share what you are sorry for – and then to hear that others feel the same.

Another session collected 'Most important issues'. The Youth group said: "The police issue is the main problem. Police abuse power towards the young and are prejudiced. For example, young people are assumed to be drunk even if sober." But they also said: "There is stereotyping both ways – youth stereotype the police too."

How do we achieve active democracy?

How do we remedy the flaws so as to achieve the outcomes described in the second? We need to:

- Make it easy for people to take part in discussing issues that concern them.
- Make sure that these discussions help people to form their opinions, because they consist of dialogue not debate.
- Create structures so that these discussions have influence.
- Legitimise decisions.

Making it easy for people to take part: In encouraging participation, politicians tend to think in terms of structures ('Let's strengthen parish councils') because they spend so much of their time inside them. But what Oscar Wilde said of socialism applies to politics in general – it takes up too many evenings. So we must concentrate in the first place not on structures but on issues. Make it easy for people to take part on the issues they care about. Recognise that many of these issues are local and environmental – and as many as 12,000 people wrote to protest about an incinerator proposed for Guildford.

Helping people to form their opinions: A citizen's jury consists typically of 16 people, invited to be representative of the community. They spend around four days hearing presentations from witnesses, helped by one or two independent moderators. At the end, the jury draws up its conclusions in a report. The number of local authorities in Britain using citizen's juries rose from less than 20 in 1991 to 110 in 1997.

I have found some accounts of juries in action very moving. This story shows vividly the difference between debate and dialogue. During one citizen's jury on health, a woman described the scene round her kitchen table from the night before: "I looked around the table at my kids and husband. Everyone was talking and no-one was listening to anyone else; not like here when we all listen and take it in turns. I told them we should all be listening to each other, and my husband laughed and said, 'Don't worry, kids; your mum has been doing a citizens' jury.... She'll be back to normal soon'."

In 1994, 300 people spent a weekend in Manchester deliberating on crime. The proportion agreeing that the courts should send fewer people to prison rose from 29 to 44 per cent during the weekend. One participant, Carmel Meredith, said: "What I liked about it is that we have covered such a wide range of opinions, that the opinion furthest away from me has made me think and strengthened my own opinion."

Creating structures so that discussions have influence: These are NEF's proposals for the way in which issues should be handled. There are three or four stages.

- *Citizen initiative:* In some cases, issues will be raised by politicians. But it is vital that citizens should also be able to raise issues. If a petition signed by one per cent of the Swiss electorate is submitted calling for a referendum on some issue currently under consideration by government, then a referendum has to be held. The signatures of two per cent of the voters are enough to call a vote on any other issue not yet under governmental consideration.
- *Deliberation for all:* I described above the National Issues Forums approach from America. We think that, impressive as these are, it is possible to go further – to make deliberation something that people can organise for themselves. How this can be done is described below.
- *Deliberations that take or influence decisions:* As I explained above, the citizens jury and the deliberative poll involve fewer people than methods like National Issues Forums, but have the advantage of being representative. I do not mean that participants represent others, as politicians do. I mean that they are similar to the group concerned with the issue. In the deliberative poll on crime, the presence of people with criminal records was one way in which that group represented society at large.

For several reasons, we need to combine deliberation for all with larger, more formal, events, probably involving a representative group. First, the larger events, however big – Washington DC's second Citizen's Summit brought 3,500 people together in 2001 – can involve only a small proportion of the total population. Secondly, the more informal stage helps people who may not feel very articulate to develop their voice and to feel more confident about getting more involved. Thirdly, deliberation can make an initially representative sample unrepresentative by the end of the process.

There may be a fourth stage, which is to legitimise the decision, maybe by holding some sort of referendum (see below).

Legitimising decisions: The previous stages may be enough to legitimise decisions. If not, a referendum may be needed. Under the Local Government Act 1972, six voters can call a parish meeting and if at least ten people turn up and call for a referendum on a local issue, the parish council is obliged to hold one, though the results are only advisory. We do need provision for binding referendums.

The role of politicians

The most thoughtful writer on this subject at present is John Stewart of the University of Birmingham. He argues that: "The passive concept of representation leaves little or no place for participatory democracy. There is therefore a tendency to see representative and participatory democracy as opposed. Given an active process of representation, however, representative democracy requires and is strengthened by participatory democracy. It is the role of elected representatives to aid the process of deliberation and in the end if required to balance and judge differing views."

There are therefore two roles for politicians, especially at local level. In some cases they set policy: in others they help to provide the framework in which the citizens can take decisions. With the advent of cabinet government in many local authorities, a new role is needed for backbenchers. Scrutinising the decisions taken by the cabinet is hardly enough. If councillors can get away from the macho notion that their job is all about taking tough decisions, a new role awaits in helping their citizens to come to full citizenship.

The role of the media

The role that the media could play is illustrated by the civic journalism being pioneered in America. The *Charlotte Observer*, for example, organised forums that brought readers face to face with candidates for governor and for the presidency. The paper used citizens' interests to shape its own coverage. One journalist said: "We weren't just a newspaper anymore, we were the electorate." When it ran stories on inner city crime, it pledged to stick with the story for at least a year and to work with the affected neighbourhoods to find solutions.

Democs stands for 'deliberative meetings organised by citizens'. It is a game that allows any group that wishes to play and, in doing so, to work through an issue of public policy.

Democs probably works best for important issues that people feel strongly about – but not too strongly. It probably helps if people's views are neither too fixed or too strong, since there won't always be a facilitator. People are more likely to want to take part where they can have an influence, so Democs will also work best where there is an obvious organisation to make use of the results. It therefore helps if policy is fluid. It will also make for a better game if there are a small number of basic policy positions.

The issues could be international, national or local. Our first four games concern four issues in human genetics: stem cell research, pre-implantation genetic diagnosis, genetic testing for insurance, and xeno-transplantation. They are being developed with funding from the Wellcome Trust.

We also want Democs to be used for lots of local issues. This marvellous quote from Edmund Burke reminds us why this is important: "To be attached to the subdivision, to love the little platoon we belong to in society, is the first principle, the germ, as it were, of public affections. It is the first link in the series by which we proceed toward a love to our country and to mankind."

Democs may be initiated by the agency responsible for an issue, or by citizens who challenge it to convene a Democ. Agreement involves the organisation:

- Committing itself on the use it will make of the results.
- Negotiating what quality thresholds it expects in return, in terms of who comes and how the meetings are run.
- Arranging for the content material to be provided.

Written material is provided about the issue. It would be certified as balanced by a neutral body such as the Electoral Reform Society or by a group of stakeholders. The material is broken down into component parts: values, statistics, proposals etc. These are on cards the size of playing cards.

Individual meetings are convened either by individual citizens or by organisations. They could be a group of friends meeting in someone's home, an alternative to quiz night in the pub, part of a public meeting, or part of the meeting of an established group like the

Women's Institute. People play in groups of six or so.

Let me give you a flavour of what it feels like to take part in a trial on our first subject, stem cell research. Everyone starts by introducing themselves. The facilitator introduces the guidelines for a good conversation. One, for example, is *'Seek the wisdom of the group –* together we have far more knowledge and wisdom than any of us can have alone. You can always learn from others however far apart you appear to be.'* Everyone uses sticky dots to vote on the four main policy positions. The facilitator then deals out the fact cards and asks the participants what basic facts they need to know to start a discussion. Someone might ask: 'So what's a stem cell then?' – and they're off. Everyone contributes from the cards in their hand: everyone gets to ask basic questions without looking stupid.

Next, people explore the range of issues that they feel are relevant to deciding policy on stem cell research. Some groups have emphasised the quality of regulation. Others have questioned whether the money could be better spent on third world diseases. Some people make links to IVF, others to abortion, yet others to human cloning. Once this range has been explored, the group tries to find areas of common ground.

Finally, participants reflect on what they've learned and whether they have identified any dilemmas in their own thinking. They vote again on the policy positions, so that everyone can see what shifts there have been. They fill in a questionnaire to help NEF learn. The whole process takes an hour and a half to two hours.

Perry Walker, co-ordinator of the Centre for Participation and Democracy at the New Economics Foundation.

Chapter 4

Education

Through my classroom window
lovers argue in mime, teaching
sorrow like rainfall

Making education human-scale
Satish Kumar

The fundamental problem of schools in general – and British schools in particular – is that they have become large, cumbersome and bureaucratic management structures, rather than learning communities. Because of their structures, schools resemble more knowledge factories than learning communities.

The nature of learning community is such that students, teachers and parents know each other intimately, support each other continuously and treat each other in a respectful and intimate manner. In knowledge factories, pupils are treated as numbers, parents are treated as interfering distractions and teachers are treated as instruments of delivering results and outcomes. Achieving goals, set by external bodies such as governments, corporations and business interests become of primary importance and caring for the true development of the pupil becomes secondary.

If we wish to transform such systems of schooling then we need to return to human scale of schools. Rather than being guided by the economy, equipment and infrastructure, schools need to be guided by the quality of interaction between pupils, teachers, parents and local community. It means that schools need to be responsive to neighbourhoods, villages and localities.

Numbers of pupils in any such school can vary from a couple of hundred to four or five hundred but no more, and such schools should be within safe walking distance, so that parents are not required to bring their children to school by car, creating congestion on the road, nor should there be any need for buses transporting children from one community to another. If a school is not rooted within a community or a neighbourhood, it cannot develop a sense of belonging to the place, nor can it become a community in itself.

Many wealthy parents, who can afford the fees, prefer to send their children to smaller schools, with smaller classes where teachers and pupils have a more informal, creative and spontaneous relationship. In such an atmosphere pupils are at ease with themselves and, therefore, can gain a deeper understanding of themselves and the world around them.

When the school is a community, then it is possible to organise its epistemology, its curriculum, and its syllabus in a holistic and interconnected way. In such a situation, teachers, pupils and parents are participants in a mutual discovery of meaning. In the context of community and with sense of belonging, knowledge is not merely intellectual information, it is also an experience of relationships – with oneself, with the natural world and with other human beings.

Such relationships go beyond academic pursuit. They enable practical and physical as much as mental, emotional and spiritual engagement. Teachers, pupils and parents work together as partners, they have time for gardening, cooking, eating together, cleaning and maintaining the school and celebration of seasons, festivals and life itself.

All such concepts will be alien to the system of knowledge factories, where large numbers are children are crammed together. Knowledge factories treat children as empty vessels to be filled with external knowledge and information, mostly through academic means, but in a learning community education becomes what it is – its original meaning – to bring out, lead out, unfold and discover what is already there in the aptitude of the pupil.

In this holistic view of the child, they come to this world with full potential. Like an acorn has the potential to be an oak tree, each and every pupil has the potential to be him or herself, but is often crushed in the bureaucratic, large, knowledge factories where the original and true potential is often ignored, forgotten or even suppressed.

The current education system expects children to become part of the system if it needs lawyers, engineers, doctors or whatever. It means that pupils are cajoled, forced and pressed to follow that particular career, so education is turned upside down. Rather than it being a voyage of self discovery, it becomes a ladder for careerism.

So return to scale in the context of education is to look at the schools as learning communities and not as knowledge factories.

This was the challenge I faced. Having two children of my own, I wondered how should they be educated? I lived in the village of Hartland, in North Devon. When my children were coming to secondary school age I realised that the nearest secondary school was 15 miles away. One was in Bude, in Cornwall, south of Hartland and the other in Bideford, east of Hartland. To send my children to either of these alternatives was no alternative. Both schools had 800-1,000 children, both required an hour's journey in the morning and an hour's journey in the evening.

A school bus travelled through a number of villages in the countryside, and it took that amount of time. So every day, five days a week and 40 weeks a year my children would have to commute, which meant a commuter's life from the age of 11. Then, if they went to those schools, they would be stuck all day in their classroom. No gardens, no kitchen where pupils could prepare their meals. Eating mass-produced food, with little taste or nutrition, was not the prospect either myself or my children relished.

So I took up the challenge and said: why don't we start a school in our own village, which is a learning community? After consulting with my neighbours and friends, it became clear that there were parents of nine pupils prepared to send their children to such a school, if it ever started. I was encouraged, and eventually established the Small School in Hartland.

On the very first day, everybody agreed that the kitchen would be the centre of the school. Preparing and sharing the meals would be as much a part of the curriculum as learning English, science, maths and music. When pupils cook the lunch now, they are not missing any lesson. Cooking is their lesson for that day and the kitchen is as much a classroom as the classroom, where French, physics and photography is taught.

As time passed more pupils joined. We created a garden. We introduced outdoor learning and learning by doing. Ecology, spirituality, community and caring of animals and plants became as much part of education as passing the GCSE exams. We decided not to exceed the numbers of pupils over 40. That seemed to be the right number for this particular neighbourhood.

As news spread, many other parents and teachers wanted to start similar schools, but how to fund such schools? We in Hartland somehow managed to raise charitable grants and public donations which complemented parental contribution. No child was turned away from the small school because of economic reasons. But not everybody can manage to raise funds in this way. We attracted funds because the Small School was seen as an example, a model that could be emulated in other places, but we realised that without state funding for such schools it would be difficult if not impossible to establish schools of this nature.

If you make the schools selective and fee-paying, and run it on the style of public schools, then it is no longer a community school. Whereas the idea behind the Small School was that any child living in that neighbourhood, irrespective of intellectual or financial background should be able to attend.

The British Prime Minister and successive education secretaries have spoken about the importance of autonomy and diversity in schools. They have talked about giving power and allowing initiative within local communities. If they were true to their word and their commitment, then they should give financial support to such non-selective, non-fee paying community schools. It is a common practice in Denmark and the Netherlands, where if parents, pupils and teachers come together and start a school then up to 80 per cent of expenditure is met by the state.

This has been practised in those two countries for decades and the schools run under such schemes are successful. If Denmark and Holland can do it why not Britain? Let us return to human scale education and we will see that many of the problems of bureaucracy, overwork, lack of discipline, teacher's stress and bullying will become more manageable. They might even disappear.

Satish Kumar is the editor of *Resurgence* magazine and a leading light of Schumacher College.

Chapter 5

Energy

I find black rocks on
a dead volcano, sun soaked
they are warm to hold

Bringing it back home
James Marriott

Greater London imports 20 million tonnes of oil equivalent per year. That's 100 super tankers of crude oil being burnt by our capital city every 12 months – more than the fuel consumption of Portugal or Denmark.

As part of two distinct but linked organisations, RENUE and PLATFORM, I am engaged in trying to tackle the problem of climate change and energy consumption from the ground-up in my home – London and the tidal Thames Valley. From this work I have begun to see three strategies that can be used in parallel:

- Installing renewable energy systems in the existing urban fabric.
- Pushing for a major reduction in overall energy use.
- Finding ways of reining in what we might call 'the carbon-industrial-complex.'

RENUE stands for Renewable Energy in the Urban Environment. Central to its work is the question: how do we make, or rather remake, sections of urban fabric or neighbourhoods in London that are adapted to meet climate change?

We all know the public targets that have been set. The UK government draft paper on climate change calls for a 10 per cent reduction of CO_2 by 2010, a 20 per cent reduction by 2020 and a 60 per cent reduction by 2050. These targets have been reinforced by strong statements by Tony Blair made in October 2000 and March 2001. The UK is also bound by EU commitments to raise the percentage of electricity generated by renewables from its current level of 2.5 per cent to 10 per cent by 2010.

Even if we hold to these targets and do not concern ourselves with the more realistic target of a 90 per cent reduction in CO2 by 2040 called for by Dr Mayer Hillman (PSI, 1995), how are we going to reach them on a local basis? What is meant by a local basis? Should they be tackled on a local rather than a purely national basis?

I find the following maxim instructive: 'Power is the ability to make sure that others carry the burdens of change.' At present, the UK is able to trumpet its achievement of having met the Kyoto targets. But, as is well known, this is simply because of 'the dash for gas', a politically and commercially motivated shift from coal-fired power stations to gas-fired power stations. We might celebrate the change that is manifested in the reduction of the UK's CO2 emissions, but the ex-mining communities of South Wales, Nottinghamshire and Yorkshire have carried the burden of this. Now we are embroiled in the process of making communities in Cornwall, Scotland and Mid-Wales carry a different burden through the construction of large wind farms.

Shouldn't all the communities of the UK carry the burden of change? Shouldn't all of us involve ourselves in the physical and practical changes required to meet the challenge of energy conservation and climate change? What happens if we start at home?

Starting at home – which is what RENUE is trying to do – is extremely difficult. RENUE's area of concern – its home – is the Lower Wandle Valley, which runs through parts of the London boroughs of Wandsworth and Merton.

The River Wandle was a source of local renewable energy from the 7th to the mid-20th centuries. It powered something like 60 watermills along its nine and a half miles, as it ran from Croydon and Carshalton through Merton down to the Thames at Wandsworth. At the perimeters of its valley, for example on Wimbledon and Wandsworth Commons, were dotted a number of windmills.

From the first decades of the 19th century, the low-carbon economy of the valley began to transform. Coal was imported in huge quantities from the Northumbrian coalfields via the wharves at the Wandle's mouth. The coal was initially imported for steam engines, and by the 1830s for a coke gas works, and by the 1900s a coal-fired power station. A great swathe of housing swept down the valley between the 1860s and 1910s: houses built cheaply on an abundance of coal, built on the assumption that this was an everlasting resource. This meant that the houses were invariably poorly insulated and had a coal-burning grate in each room.

Today this pattern of energy used in the valley continues, deriving from carbon sources in distant parts. Electricity comes to light homes in Wandsworth via the National Grid. At any one time, this energy may be generated at power stations that burn coal dug from South Wales, Yorkshire, South Africa, West Virginia and so on. The gas that fuels cookers in Merton may at any one time be drawn from the North Sea, Siberia, Algeria – or even further afield.

This global system of energy leads not only to insecurity of supply, but also to the user not knowing the provenance of their fuel. This lack of knowledge means that the fuel lacks meaning for the user. When you brew a cup of fair trade coffee, compare the meaning that you instil in the drink, compared with the lack of meaning that you instil in the gas or electricity that heats the water.

RENUE's work of installing renewable energy systems in new and existing buildings in the Lower Wandle Valley is not only about generating low-carbon fuel, or about reducing continent-spanning fuel systems, but also crucially about reconnecting people with the provenance of their energy. RENUE has been working to create a solar-powered pub, a solar-assisted school and further education college, a solar-assisted row of shops, a water-power assisted junior school and a Renewable Energy and Community Resource Centre – but this work can be very difficult to realise.

How many renewable energy systems can you name in London? There are a number of examples of renewable technologies installed but many are not operational. There are a wide variety of schemes – designed, planned and desired, but many are not yet realised. The London Research Centre's publication *Renewable Energy in London*, published in 2000, paints a comprehensive picture, but the overall number of operational schemes remains pitiful.

Why is this so? Partly due to finance, as there is a commercial return to be made on those distant wind farms but no profit to be derived from solarising a 19th century school building in inner-London. Less obviously, the key obstacle that RENUE has faced derives from land – its ownership, the ownership of buildings, the active turnover of these commodities in the city and the profit to be made out of this market. These are issues seemingly far from the question of climate change that have a key impact on the way that people – landowners, homeowners or tenants – will think about the long term and install renewable systems for the long term.

Why have so few of us installed a solar water heater or photo-voltaic panel on our house, office or flat? Why have we not lobbied to have these systems installed on our children's schools or our favourite pub? The answer may well lie in the fact that we don't think about these buildings and our sense of ownership over them over the long- term – a detached, short-term mind-set which is a feature of contemporary metropolitan life.

The second strategy, 'working for a major reduction in overall energy use', I find engages me on a less institutional and more individual and personal level. I am absolutely immersed in a high carbon lifestyle. Dr Mayer Hillman, who I mentioned earlier, puts it succinctly:

> "On a per capita basis the UK needs to cut its carbon emissions by over 90 per cent – i.e. a 5 per cent annual reduction from now until 2040... What does this mean for a typical household with its current annual emissions of over 25 tonnes? Each household's share of power station and refinery emissions is about 11 tonnes, industry 5.5 tonnes, domestic heating 3.5 tonnes, and transport 4.5 tonnes. A ration of 2.5 tonnes would only stretch to the most essential of activities. Flying across the Atlantic would use up a large part of this."

I ask myself, how much more energy do I use up at the age of 37 than my father did aged 37 in 1967? Or my grandfather in 1937? I think of the motor vehicles, flying, trains, electrical appliances, synthetic fabrics and plastics from hydrocarbons, and so on. I know intuitively that the scale of my energy usage is way above what would be ecologically just, but when Hillman talks of a 90 per cent reduction over a period of 45 years that's an extraordinary cut back year on year. How much have I decreased my personal energy use this year, when measured against last year? How do I measure it?

How is this kind of change to come about? It is certainly difficult to persuade others to think and act on these matters – loft lagging is about the least sexy thing you can do. But I can begin with myself and try to find the pleasure that might come through altering the patterns of my life. There is no reason for me to suppose that my father at 37 was any more or less happy than I am. Or likewise my grandfather. But I can be sure that their contribution to CO2 emissions was substantially less – we can surely 'de-link' energy use from happiness. Or to use a maxim from Gandhi 'renounce and enjoy.'

The third strategy is 'finding ways of reining in what we might call 'the carbon-industrial-complex''. When we think of the world's oil cities, we might think of Dallas, Kuwait, Baku – we probably do not think about London. There are no oilfields on the city fringes, but our metropolis not only consumes those 100 super tankers of crude per year, it is also home to two of the three largest oil corporations in the world – BP Amoco and Shell.

In this era of outsourcing, these trans-nationals are not hermetic structures – they depend crucially upon other companies and organisations to enable them to function. For example BP's global accounting is carried out by PriceWaterhouseCoopers; Ogilvy and Mather carry out its global advertising. Stretched across our city is a web of individuals that drive forward an industry that extracts oil, coal and gas and brings them to the marketplace where all of us purchase and burn them. London is like a vast machine that pulls carbon from the lithosphere and thrusts it into the atmosphere.

How is this industrial-carbon-complex to be reigned in? This is a pressing question for our locality, because it is here – not in Nigeria, Azerbaijan or West of Shetland – that this complex is most intense and active. Our home offers us an almost unique opportunity to address this question head-on.

Perhaps one day there will be a massive redirection of capital from the carbon industry into renewables and energy efficiency measures. I am inspired by the history of our city. After the catastrophe of the Fire of London, funds had to be found to raise up a new St Paul's Cathedral. Finance for an edifice that would not generate a direct return on capital, but that was essential for civic pride and virtue. A new tax was instituted specifically to pay for St Paul's – a tax on coal imported at London's wharves.

James Marriott is a founding member of the PLATFORM arts and campaign group.

Chapter 6

Food

Here are two apples
in one I smell the meadow
the second, nothing

Re-localising what we eat
Vicki Hird

Few issues have hit the headlines as consistently as food during the last decade. For fair reason or foul – or fowl in some cases – policies and practices in the food and farming sector have regularly sparked public debates about how we produce food. The latest animal disease, foot-and-mouth, and the draconian measures used to eradicate it, whipped this debate into a media frenzy.

Obviously the costly nature of our farming is attacked, £3 billion to subsidise the farm sector, £4 billion to sort out BSE, and probably another £4 billion to sort out foot and mouth. Other costs are being realised. Who picks up the tab for cleaning up pesticides and nitrate pollution? Healthcare costs for the thousands of cases of food- and diet-related disease runs into billions. Diet-related diseases, such as some cancers, obesity and coronary heart disease kill thousands each year and most are on the increase.

Food miles have been shown not only to contribute to traffic on the roads, but also spread of disease and loss of integrity and traceability within the food chain. As the recent report *Eating Oil* showed, our heavy reliance on fuel for our food supplies makes the food system highly inefficient, unsustainable and very vulnerable. Also under scrutiny is the role of the highly and increasingly concentrated food retail sector in forcing down prices to farmers yet maintaining prices in the shops.

Last but not least are the agriculture and trade policies that influence what is grown where. The £40 billion spent on agricultural subsidies via the European Common Agricultural Policy, for instance, could be far better used to support green farming and rural development. The current CAP subsidy system also encourages over-production of unhealthy products like sugar and animal fats and these make their way, often by manufacturers' stealth, into people's diets.

Internationally, the rules on such subsidies are being discussed but where the rhetoric on stopping rotten subsidies systems are good, the pace of change is either slow or entirely in the wrong direction. This is especially so in the USA, where President Bush recently agreed to a huge increase in subsidies going mostly to corporate farming interests. Meanwhile, developing countries suffer from a hugely unfair playing field and cannot get out of the debt cycle we have put them on.

So questions are being asked about the fundamental future of farming in the UK. In what form can it survive recurrent crises and increased global food trading? Further intensification with a bit of organic on the side, or a wholesale restructuring of food supply and demand?

The key to the long-term future of food production is to look at the system as a whole. In an ideal world, a sound food and farm policy should work for farming and rural communities, the environment and biodiversity, farm animals, consumers and public health, and for countryside users. It must also not threaten food security, sustainable agriculture or food economies elsewhere, especially in developing countries.

Such a vision can be achieved. The shopper's power can be mighty – witness the fall of genetically modified foods and the rise of organic. Joined-up government thinking is needed on rural, food, faming, competition, public health, transport and planning policies. Change will rely on farmers co-operating and consumers choosing to eat fewer but better livestock products, more local and fresh foods rather than convenience and fast food.

This return to scale will not be rapid, as the systems we currently rely on are huge behemoths, which will resist change. The big food companies and retailing multiples have invested heavily in centralised distribution, 'efficient customer response', and international supply chains. But in reality, even they are already beginning to see how reliance on ever fewer suppliers, on ever longer supply chains and ever more remote producers, incurs risks. Ultimately, they will want to reduce the risk. But in the meantime what we must see is a renewal in the alternatives to these great food giants.

We do this by building up capacity both as consumers to use primary produce rather than pre-packed meals or fast food and as traders in trading directly with producers at local shops, farmers markets, farm shops and cooperatives. We will also need to press for specific measures so that these outlets survive, thrive and grow in numbers.

Local food

It is worth giving a definition of what local food is about. It is about bringing together the competing interests in the food chain and ensuring that a consensus is developed locally about what sort of food system people need in the future. The result should be a rich diversity of practical projects: festivals, markets, directories, cook books, school projects and cookery clubs.

Meanwhile, a growing number of businesses are turning their back on the global supermarket and joining together to protect and create local food economies in which producers, processors, caterers and retailers work together to produce and process food as close to the point of consumption as possible. It is also about health, environment, community, economy, education and ethical trading.

The recent recommendations of Prime Minister Tony Blair's Policy Commission of the Future of Farming and Food certainly recognised the need for a return to scale. They said:

> "Local food markets could deliver on all aspects of sustainable development – economic (by providing producers with a profitable route to market), environmental (by cutting down on the pollution associated with food transportation, and by interesting consumers in how the land around them is farmed), and social (by encouraging a sense of community between buyer and seller, town and country."

They could not sadly translate that into real recommendations but we can do that. Ten things that need to be done:

- *Integrate the whole food system:* DEFRA should work with all departments to make sure that changes are made, understood and accepted – however painfully – by all sectors. This will require joined-up thinking across government departments.

- *Work with EU partners to really reform the Common Agricultural Policy:* The presence of Green farm ministers in Europe provides the perfect chance to put root-and-branch reform of the CAP onto the agenda in Brussels and Geneva. Tony Blair must work to turn the rhetoric of support for green farming into reality by converting all CAP production support into an integrated – and, dare I say it, more nationally designed – rural and farm development policy. Right now, the UK should have a target for converting the first aim of the CAP, production support, to the second aim, rural development and green farming measures. The new approach could be based on simple, whole farm management agreements – paying farmers and rural businesses for specific actions and results, based on sustainable production. European food regulations too have been criticised. They must protect society but also create thriving local food chains.

- *Encourage local production for local consumption:* We urgently need shorter food chains, more local abattoirs and processing facilities and a diverse retailing sector. This will all rely on new and better cross-departmental policy initiatives. These include consumer campaigns, grants for marketing and skills development, logistical and operational support for local enterprises, promotion of farmers' markets and direct buying schemes and pushing for regional sourcing by retailers.

- *Promote and protect ecological and public health:* It is time to stop the thinking that places environmental and conservation objectives into a different box to consumer and public health objectives. They are intimately entwined. For instance, reducing the mix and level of agro-chemicals in the food chain is a mutual objective – good for farms as well as for reducing food residues. Producing foods more locally should reduce food miles and give consumers fresher produce. Reducing the distances travelled by animals has clear benefits for human, animal and environmental health, as the foot-and-mouth outbreak showed. Food poisoning is on the increase and new problems are on the horizon, such as bugs resistant to antibiotics. Better regulations must reduce such hazards and improve standards along the whole global food chain. Internationally, the Codex Alimentarius Commission, which sets international food standards, needs wholesale reform to make sure trade rules enhance food safety and quality, rather than undermine them by using lowest common denominators to set standards.

- *Set a target and action plan for organic food and farming:* We're half way there with an action plan being developed by DEFRA and key stakeholders. But it needs targets and it needs to result in action so that we can reap the benefits of more local organic farming.

- *Ensure healthy diets for all:* Stopping over-production of unhealthy foods and enhancing production of healthy foods like fruit and vegetables must be a priority. Over 10 per cent of UK consumers also can't afford healthy diets – they lack the minerals and vitamins to maintain good health or the healthy development of children and unborn babies. There are three main factors behind this food poverty: financial access, physical access and access to information. A revised minimum income standard must be set so that tax and other benefits are properly linked to what is required for a decent standard of living and a good diet. Government must guarantee healthy meals in schools and hospitals and increase access to information about what constitutes a healthy diet. We must be developing policies that improve physical access, including promoting local food production, and should be enhancing community food projects such as community orchards and allotments.

- *Put animal welfare at the heart of policy:* For food safety, quality, environmental and ethical reasons, we should have a food policy based on stronger animal welfare standards. Ending the long-distance transport of animals and battery farming must be political imperatives, but we also need to promote more extensive livestock practices through support, training for farm workers and grants.

- *Internalise the costs of the food chain that are now paid by the public purse, consumers and innocent third parties:* The costs of unsustainable production on society are great: some conservative studies suggest £2.3 billion a year for cleaning up pollution and so on. To guide all those involved in the food chain away from chemically intensive farming and long distance food systems, we need economic disincentives to pollute through energy and pesticide taxes and positive incentives to get off the chemical treadmill.

- *More investment in the right kind of research:* Evidence-based policy is a must. We must not continue to fail to invest in research, fail to produce evidence, and then interpret the absence of evidence of risk as if it were evidence of the absence of risk. To make sure that we have a clear view, we must invest in research into all approaches to food production, including sustainable methods, such as organic farming, as well as carrying out research into shortening the food chain.

- *Get retail competition working for society:* The loss of independent retailers and wholesalers and the increase in market share of the major food retail multiples has caused numerous problems. Suppliers are compelled to sell to the multiples and to comply with their standards and demands. Low-income families lose food options, as local stores cannot compete with the multiples. Local authorities, regional development agencies and other stakeholders must assess local and regional needs for retail and food supply so that local monopolies do not develop and local food economies are rebuilt. Again, it is the whole food chain that matters. In the interim, the government must act to make sure farmers get a fair deal for all of their produce by implementing a strong, legally binding code of practice.

In reality, as even some of the biggest international food processors have realised, only a sustainable food production system – in terms of soil, climate change, toxins, transport and so on – will provide the food and therefore the profits in the future. The reasons for a return to scale are simple, but the changes required are complex and difficult. Good practice exists and needs replicating locally, regionally and nationally to deliver the far better food we deserve.

Vicki Hird is policy director of Sustain: the alliance for better food and farming which has 105 organisations working together to reform agriculture and food policy and practice. She is the author of *Perfectly Safe to Eat: The Facts on Food* (Women's Press) and is also a member of the Farm Animal Welfare Council and a director of the Food Commission and Growing Communities – a food growing and buying enterprise in north London.

Chapter 7

Health

And when she touched me
this pain went faster than
with any pill

Why professionals need patients
Sarah Burns

The National Health Service is currently facing a conundrum. There are huge amounts of money being pumped into improving the service: in the 2000 budget, the government announced an unprecedented increase in NHS funding of 6.1 per cent average annual real terms growth over the four years to 2003-04 – the longest period of sustained high growth in the history of the NHS. But even this seems unable to reduce the waiting lists, iron out discrepancies between different areas or improve people's perception of the service.

Most significantly, spending money on health services alone doesn't seem to make us any healthier or happier. In fact, in the recent lecture at the London School of Economics Professor Richard Layard said that "all the evidence suggests that clinical depression has increased since the Second World War."

That is because delivering good health is not just about coming up with technical solutions to ill-health – more pills, more screening and more operations. These things are important, but they are not the heart of the matter. Instead, good health is about getting the broader determinants of health right – finding work you enjoy doing, having access to good quality housing and most importantly feeling like you are in control of your life and your destiny.

One famous Whitehall study showed that, as civil servants moved up and down the management hierarchy, their arteries clogged and unclogged. The more autonomy and control they had in their everyday life, the healthier they were but as they moved down the scale and lost control their arteries gradually clogged up.

This isn't news. The Alma Ata Declaration on Primary Health Care of 1978, which was endorsed by all the countries of the world, sought to instate people as the prime movers for shaping their health services and strengthen the capacity of people to cope with

49

their own health problems, rather than starting with various types of health technologies and considering people as their passive recipients.

The declaration considered health as an integral whole and called for social control of the health services so that they helped to strengthen people's coping capacity. Alma Ata was part of a global health movement that included the development of `Barefoot Doctors' in China and helped to kick-start the whole public health movement.

Since the 1970s, though, this broader understanding of health – with local people at the heart of making it happen – has taken some knocks. People are now described more as health consumers rather than active producers of good health. We are obsessed with having the latest health technologies – as much as we are obsessed by having the latest handbag or the latest car. In January 2003, Alan Milburn gave a speech in which he used the increase of prescribing rates as a measure of good performance within the NHS – which just goes to show how twisted our notions of good health have become, when we think the amount of drugs we take is a measure of good health.

The rising power of pharmaceutical conglomerates hasn't helped either. If we believed their marketing hype, we'd be able to take a pill to cure every ailment. And yet we know in our heart of hearts that pills are not enough.

Yet at the heart of this new consumer movement for health there are the potential seeds of a healthy renaissance – with people and community back centre stage taking control of their own health and creating the conditions for healthier people and planet. The signs are there: NHS reform which is all about 'shifting the balance of power,' primary care trusts that are meant to be about local people taking control of the local health agenda, and Foundation Hospitals which reduce control from central government. There are even new organisations called patient forums to ensure patients get a voice in creating a vision and strategy for local health.

Not only do the opportunities exist – but there are also plenty of practical examples of people-centred health already working on the ground.

Manchester Primary Care Trust has come up with a groundbreaking approach to jointly commissioning services with the local community. Local Area Groups or LAGS bring together trust directors with local people to come up with ways of tackling problems – like rising rates of post-natal depression. The purpose of LAGs is to come up with practical solutions to problems that won't go away. The LAGs which have worked best are those which have actively recognised and valued the very different perspectives and values that participants bring – rather than trying to impose a consensus. The organisers admit that bringing such different people together has been hard work but that it has enabled them to come up with solutions that really stick – in this case a new post-natal counselling service.

Faraway in rural Somerset, the health authority has come up with a similar, related approach: health panels recruit local people to help make decisions about funding priorities, and in 70 per cent of cases the decision of the panel had a direct impact upon the planning of health and social care provision. Recruitment to the panel is rotating, with each panel member taking six months to be inducted and six months to participate and help to induct the next batch of participants. In this way, experience and confidence is cascaded down and community capacity developed.

The New Economics Foundation (NEF) has worked with the Rushey Green Group Practice in Catford, South East London, to develop an innovative way of incentivising community participation – time banks. For every hour a patient gives helping the practice or giving support to others, they earn time credits through the time bank. Everyone's time is worth the same and research undertaken by researchers at St Thomas's Hospital shows that this kind of neighbourhood support can help cut visits to the GP.

The success of Rushey Green in building new mutual, community-based approaches to delivering good health has meant that the time bank idea – the idea of public services as mutual endeavours between professionals and users, rather than just one-way delivery mechanisms – has generated a lot of interest from health trusts.

The South London and Maudsley NHS Trust has launched its own mutual volunteering scheme and is using the time bank tool to start to generate community-based support for people being discharged from mental health services. One project, targeting ethnic minority groups in Peckham, is using the time bank tool to help prevent hospital admissions in the first place.

Each of these examples shows that a different approach to thinking about health *is* possible. But good examples on their own are not enough. And if we are not careful, good examples when translated into mainstream practice can become just another set of rules and performance indicators to meet. And the NHS already has enough of those.

The structures and space for people are already being created in the health service. But they are currently under-occupied because we lack the means of involving people meaningfully. If we don't come up with the tools to colonise these new spaces, they will be taken back by the system – by professional managers and bureaucrats.

So what can we do?

First of all, we must agree what involvement means – getting people to come up with problem-solving strategies – not just coming up with complaints when things have already gone wrong.

This kind of meaningful involvement means trusting people more and taking risks – something the current health service is not best equipped to do but which comparable programmes, like Sure Start have been very successful at, partly because they are run by health professionals, like health visitors who have a very strong commitment to people-centred health care. The Sure Start programme has a generally high level of involvement, with an average of 20 volunteers working on each programme and five parents represented on the management board.

It means remembering that staff need to be involved as much as patients. But it also means going further than just involving the 'experts' and coming up with a new kind of professionalism that includes what patients and ordinary people have to offer as well. As NHS chief executive Nigel Crisp suggests: "Changing mindsets from professionals doing things to or for patients to doing things with them... engendering mutual respect between patients and professionals, different groups and management."

It means remembering that health works best when people become active co-producers rather than passive consumers and using every opportunity to ask people to make a contribution of time, energy or knowledge.

It means finding ways to reward and incentivising these kinds of contributions. Not just taking a free ride on people's time as we currently do – for example the 6.5 billion hours of informal care provided by carers (the Office of National Statistics estimate this time is worth £13.9 billion) – time that is largely unrecognised and unvalued but without which health and social care services would collapse.

It is also about creating a new kind of human scale health institution, which people can relate to and feel at home in rather than dwarfed and intimidated by. People live their lives in communities and neighbourhoods and our health organisations should reflect that.

Finally, let's not forget all the other people who have a role in determining health – educators, local government officials, local business. Why not provide real incentives, like extra resources or additional freedoms for all those agencies who have the imagination and will to dream up schemes that cross boundaries and sectors and really help to solve intransigent health problems – like how to get older people home from hospital.

The bottom line is that we need to create new kinds of local participation and ownership to really mainstream and establish a people-centred health service.

The Rushey Green Group Practice may have hit upon a new kind of mutual health enterprise that does just that. The practice is in the process of negotiating a new kind of contract with the time bank – an agreement to the effect that the time bank will help them to deliver health outcomes, like getting the rate of teenage pregnancy down and cutting emergency admissions to A&E for diabetes sufferers – which they on their own, with their prescriptions and their expertise are unable to achieve.

They have recognised that they need the community to help them reach their health targets and they are willing to create new kinds of mutual health enterprises, so that the community and the practice gets there together.

Local health commissioners need similar freedoms and leaps of imagination. They need to starts trusting local people enough to develop real partnerships that involve the community as co-producers. Without this, the health service will fail to deliver real health gains – despite, in fact *because*, of the huge input from money and 'professionals'.

Sarah Burns is head of the people and public services programme at the New Economics Foundation.

Chapter 8

Money

*All those coins the same
dull metal clunks, like a
one note symphony*

**The lure of gold
David Boyle**

My parents live in a little village called Nether Wallop. A generation ago it managed to boast two shops, a post office, two pubs, a butchers, a village policeman, a doctor and district nurse, and a railway station – connected to a massive local rail network – only a couple of miles away.

That was during the Austerity years of the 1940s. Now, when we are incomparably 'richer', all that's left is one pub and a very occasional bus. The conventional reasons for this – low taxes, over-regulation, fat cat salaries – don't really explain why, despite unprecedented prosperity, it seems so hard to afford the simplest public services, health, post and education.

So why aren't politicians asking about this? First, the critique of money-creation for most of the 20th century came from the political right. It was Roosevelt's opponent Huey Long in the 1930s who exemplified the idea, later assassinated.

In the UK, the social credit movement regarded themselves as part of a wider reform movement that wanted a strong central state. So much so that they marched in the 1930s, a bit like Mosley, but as the Greenshirts.

The Greenshirts emerged as a breakaway movement from the Boy Scouts and in turn gave birth to the Woodcraft Folk. How that could transmute into a militaristic organisation dedicated to currency reform is anyone's guess – but that's another story.

That is the first reason. Money reform seemed tinged with fascism – especially as social credit unravelled into an unpleasant mix of paranoia and anti-semitism – nothing like its exponents who have revived the best of Major Douglas' ideas today.

The second reason is that, actually, shortage of money isn't really the problem. If you flooded the world with money, we know exactly what would happen to it. With a rush of wind, like the Wicked Witch of the East, it would shoot into the City of London and Wall Street. And there still wouldn't be enough where it's really needed. That seems to me to be the key problem, and the reason why the old money reform movements won't work any more.

Keynes called gold a 'barbarous relic', and – especially if you look at the price of it these days – you kind of imagine the days of gold have gone for good. But we are as much in thrall to the gold mindset as we ever were.

Of course, the euro isn't the Gold Standard – but it sometimes sounds a bit like it. It's about stability of value, about strong money. It makes the same mistake as the Wizard of Oz – in it's time, a diatribe against the obsession with gold. It really *believes* in objective values, and that somehow these values can be reflected everywhere the currency circulates.

In 1925, the then Chancellor of the Exchequer Winston Churchill described a system of international currencies that "vary together, like ships in harbour whose gangways are joined and who rise and fall together with the tide".

He wasn't an early conversion to EMU. This was a description of gold standard money on the eve of our return to it. It was a famously disastrous decision, instrumental in the Great Depression and therefore in the Second World War too.

But before I take this line of argument any further, let me first say that I am a convinced and enthusiastic European. I am not a Europhobe, still less a xenophobe. But there is still a fundamental problem at the heart of the euro, and any currency based on the idea of objective values like gold. And it's this: single currencies tend to favour the rich and impoverish the poor.

They do so because changing the value of your currency, and varying your interest rate, is the way that disadvantaged places are able to make their goods more affordable. When you prevent them from doing that, you trap whole cities and regions – the poorest people in the poorest places – without being able to trade their way out.

Now of course the USA has one currency. So does Britain. But if we're honest about it, we know that hasn't been satisfactory either – because central banks set their interest rates to favour their capital cities. Eddie George, the Bank of England governor, admitted as much on the *Today* programme at Christmas 2001.

Look at the great gulfs between rich and poor in the USA. Look at the plight of cities like Detroit or states like West Virginia. And over here, look at the way interest rates are set to suit the City of London, while the manufacturing regions of the north struggle as best they can. Across a continent, the effects are so much worse. That's why Ireland's economy has been overheating, while east Germany's is languishing in poverty.

That's the danger of the euro as presently arranged, and don't underestimate it. It means success for the cities that are already successful. It means a real struggle for the great reviving cities like Newcastle and Sheffield. Different cities, different communities, value different aspects of life. And single currencies are not the universal measuring rods they claim to be.

Take, for example, Lordship Lane in Dulwich, near where I live. If you want a nail in a peculiar shape, or a weird kind of screwdriver, then you can't go wrong in Lordship Lane. Because East Dulwich has an absolute plethora of small DIY shops. They have been there since anyone can remember, and most are staffed by ancient enthusiasts who know absolutely everything anyone could possibly want to know about plastering, emulsion and brass screws.

But they and their shops are an endangered species. A plan to build a Homebase superstore on one of the last remaining bits of green nearby will probably strip Lordship Lane of this particular speciality. And although the balance sheets of Homebase will probably show a big boost, we locals will have lost something too [note: this plan was turned down in July 2003].

The question is this. Why don't these aspects of wealth show up in the figures? If money is supposed to reflect people's preferences, why doesn't it reflect the preferences of the locals? There are lots of reasons, of course, but one is that the yardstick the global players use – an international currency like the pound – doesn't measure fine mesh local wealth like that. And there's the problem: because the pound is all we've got.

Whatever your attitude to the euro, we need to think about this. Take for example, the issue of feedback. The information that relative values of currencies gives us all as they change. Of course, if there's no role for fluctuating currency values, we needn't worry about this. We can relax and let the currency traders do what they dare. But what if there is?

"Imagine a group of people who are all properly equipped with diaphragms and lungs, but share only one single brainstem breathing centre," wrote Jane Jacobs in Cities and the Wealth of Nations. "In this goofy arrangement, through breathing they would receive consolidated feedback on the carbon dioxide level of the whole group, without discriminating among the individuals producing it...

But suppose some of these people were sleeping, while others were playing tennis... Worse yet, suppose some were swimming and diving, and for some reason, such as the breaking of the surf, had no control over the timing of these submersions... In such an arrangement, feedback control would be working perfectly on its own terms, but the results would be devastating."

Currencies rising and falling in value provide us with a self-regulating feedback that lets disadvantaged areas lower their relative value. Different currencies, different interest rates, suit different cities and communities – just as they suit different sectors. This is of course also true of national currencies, but the distortion is bound to be bigger for multinational currencies like the euro. Hong Kong and Singapore had their own money, says Jane Jacobs; Detroit didn't.

Then there is the problem of complexity. In a modern economy – even in a modern city – there is really more than one economy at work. And big currencies don't suit them all very accurately. Take the sheer diversity of London. We all of us – from nurses to currency traders – have to get by using the one currency, the value of which is decided by tens of thousands of youthful traders in Wall Street and the City.

That is fine for the international economy, the financial services sector. But there's another economy in London – or Paris or Berlin – which feeds off the pickings from the rich table above it, but isn't necessarily part of it. It is the economy of the rest of us – those aspects of life which have nothing to do with financial services. The international economy brings in executives from all over the world, whose employers will pay their housing expenses no matter what – forcing up the value of London homes beyond anywhere else in the country, and pricing London services beyond the other economy.

That is why London struggles to employ nurses or teachers or bus drivers because they can't afford to live here, so the basic services suffer. We can all see the symptoms – expensive theme bars, yuppie online travel agents, but no local shops. Worse, London's rich economy threatens to drive out the poor economy completely. You can see the same thing happen in offshore financial centres where financial services have priced everything else into oblivion. In places like Jersey, it's the cuckoo in the nest.

Jersey's offshore status has made it rich after all, and yet there isn't any longer a Jersey agriculture sector to speak of, and the tourist sector is well past its prime. Why? Because nobody but bankers can afford to live and work there.

But there is a third economy in London too, and it is also threatened because we don't see it. The third economy isn't really an economy at all: it makes up the crucial human transactions that build families and neighbourhoods, look after old people, without which nothing we can do can be successful.

Economists call this 'social capital' and market forces don't apply here – people don't after all bid for food at the dinner table. Yet without it, the police can't catch criminals, doctors can't heal, children can't be educated and the other economies can't work. The futurist Alvin Toffler asks executives what it would cost their business in hard cash if their new recruits had never been toilet-trained. That's business without social capital.

This social economy doesn't appear in the GDP, so politicians assume it's inexhaustible, so they ignore it. The problem is that single currencies – whether they are the pound, the dollar or the euro – don't measure the needs and assets in these other economies very accurately.

That's the third issue we have to tackle. First feedback, then complexity and now the problem of measurement.

But then all of these are related to measurement. Big currencies don't measure very well. What they miss out gets ignored. Then it gets forgotten. Big currencies are gold-standard thinking. They condemn us all to walk around, like the people in the Emerald City, in the Wizard of Oz, wearing tinted glasses which can only recognise what the City of London and Wall Street says is important. Currencies are not just measuring systems then, they are eyeglasses. They are the way we see the world. If our currencies don't value things, we just don't see them. Then they disappear. If you only measure GDP, then the environment, human dignity, community, family all in the end get driven out. That's what faulty measuring rods do, and currencies are measuring rods.

This is the central issue of new economics – the way that global money systems drive out other cultures, other species, other opinions, other forms of wealth. That's why the New Economics Foundation exists. And that's why I say this failure of measurement, this blindness, is the real problem of money. No amount of new ways of creating it by central banks is going to solve this problem.

Different people need different kinds of money, which behave in different ways and value different assets. But we also all need different kinds of money for different aspects of our lives. If we don't get that, some parts of our cities will be rich and some poor. And some parts of our lives will be rich and some poor.

The solution isn't the euro, it is currency choice. But the paradox is that, even before we vote on the issue, currency choice is what we're going to get. Because most big retailers say they are going to accept the euro anyway. So we should welcome the euro to Britain alongside the pound. We should encourage shops to accept it – and they will. We should encourage exporters to accept it, and maybe pay their staff partly in it. We should use it as a second currency for Britain to guard us against the next generation of currency crises.

And then the euro-enthusiasts can campaign for an incremental euro, taking its place alongside the pound *because people use it* – not because it is foisted on them. We can campaign step by step for local authorities to accept payment in euros, for government to accept tax in euros, for parking meters to accept euros. That is a euro policy that suits a nation committed to internationalism, decentralisation and local control. Instead of an all-or-nothing referendum campaign, flying in the face of public opinion – with the prospect of a society even more economically divided if the government wins – we empower people to use the currency that suits them best.

Of course most people will continue to use pounds. But there will be a radical chic about using euros, and it will be strong enough for people to carry on doing so once the novelty has worn off – especially if they spend time or do business on the continent. We may even get dual pricing. And we're a sophisticated IT society now. Tills will be able to deal with this without any trouble.

But why stop there? If we need a range of yardsticks, so we need a range of currencies. Time banks to underpin the social economy. Local currencies to keep money and resources circulating locally. Regional currencies to provide low cost finance to small business. Each of them giving value to assets and resources that the big currencies can't see. Barter currencies like trade pounds can let us exchange unsold plane seats or hotel rooms or toothpaste in last year's colour, when the market doesn't recognise them as valuable.

Five million perfectly good computers are put into landfill in the UK every year. They have value – but in pounds or dollars, they're worthless. Time banks can recognise them and get them back into use.

Michael Linton, the inventor of LETS, who I'm glad to say is in the process of moving from British Columbia to Oxford, has developed a revolutionary new software that allows people – even pairs of people – to trade in an infinite number of currencies over the internet. I recommend you look at this at openmoney.org, because I think it's a real breakthrough in mutual credit.

I can imagine open money forming the basis of the London currency we need here, providing very low-cost loans to small businesses, keeping the wealth circulating here instead of dashing off around the globe to hedge funds and tax havens. Electronic currencies like that are designed to be put on smartcards, and I suggest we use the new smartcard that's about to be distributed to five million Londoners for their underground journeys.

In fact we could use the electronic money on the cards as a currency too – let's call it tubes. If a range of small businesses shared the ability to use these tube cards, then the underground could become a lender in itself – backed by the value their currency has in transport journeys. This is not money that's likely to seep out across the globe either.

As for the time currency to underpin London's voluntary sector, that's up and running already in the shape of the London Time Bank. There are now 14 time banks in London, in health centres, schools and housing estates, measuring and rewarding the effort people put in locally in a currency called time credits. In fact, you can go to the Rushey Green health centre in Catford and find yourself confronted, not by a doctor, but by a builder with a cupboard full of hacksaws and screwdrivers. Part of the small repair service, run by patients and paid for in time credits.

Time banks in London are already beginning to give value to all those assets that pounds and euros don't recognise – old people's time, young people's time, old computers and much else besides. And they are directing it at the enormous weight of unmet need in our cities: loneliness, isolation – maybe just the need to collect medicines for someone. Just as the big currencies can't recognise assets, they also have difficulty recognising needs.

I believe, within a generation or so, we will have regional currencies in most UK regions – based on the value of bonds and fluctuating against each other in value. We will have 500 mutual credit currencies underpinning small business and based on open source software. We will have at least 1,500 time currencies in health centres, schools and housing estates in every city, in regional networks – exchangeable around the country. And we will have a range of experimental currencies based on anything from renewable energy to the value of local agricultural produce.

Now people say this whole business of multiple currencies is never going to happen. It's out of a story book. It's pie in the sky. But the truth is it's happening already. I don't just mean the 7,000 or so local currencies and time banks already running in the world – or the highly successful printed currency that grew out of the Ithaca farmers market in upstate New York.

Nor do I mean the growth of electronic currencies in the shape of loyalty points. Though it's true that the latest loyalty card from Boots has space on it for more than 20 different e-currencies. And until recently Northwest Airlines used to pay their entire worldwide PR account in frequent flyer points. No, I mean the way international barter has been successfully using electronic currencies called trade dollars. In fact anything up to a fifth of world trade is now carried out in this way. And when local barter exchanges can't immediately find what they need, they use an international currency called *universal* to barter it from elsewhere.

The Wir system in Switzerland – the only survival of the local money revival in the 1930s – is now underpinning the Swiss building and restaurant industries by providing low-cost loans in a parallel currency. And they have an annual turnover equivalent to 12 billion dollars.

The business world is *already* using these currencies, and for precisely the same reason I want us to concentrate on them. Because big currencies don't measure their assets very well. And if business can do it, I don't see why the benefits shouldn't also be made available to regions, cities and communities – and I don't see how central banks can clamp down on it. Multiple currencies are here already. We can't uninvent them.

But, ah you say, what about Argentina? Argentina is an excellent example. First of why big currencies – in this case, the peso linked to the US dollar – can be disastrous. And second, why a diversity of currencies is important.

There is a problem with the regional paper currencies being issued in a flurry by local governments out there. The patacon, the lecop, the quebracho, federales, petrom. They could cause the local currency baby to be thrown out with the bathwater. That's certainly what the IMF wants. People who have lost faith in the national paper currency backed by debt are not going to be reassured by exactly the same thing issued at local level.

What Argentina needs is money that is based on something secure. On local produce. On the value of beef. On the value of local renewable energy, as suggested by Bob Swann in Massachusetts. On something you can put your faith in. You can do that if you can break away from the old idea that money is one, indivisible, totemic, semi-divine, golden truth – issued from on high by an infallible Treasury and handed down to a grateful populace. And all the solutions an increasingly frantic Washington Consensus are trying to foist on Argentina betray the same mistake.

Though the gold standard disappeared in 1931, the attitudes lying behind it are with us still – and they blind us to our own wealth. On the other hand, complementary currencies can reveal to us that, even in the poorest places, there are vast living assets – ideas, skills, time, love even – that can turn our ideas of scarcity on their heads. That is why I believe that a parallel pound and euro can show us a new way forward. It means taking the power to create money back into our own hands.

We can do it ourselves. Not by ourselves, but with each other. We can create the basis for the wealth we need. The problem is that we have little political tradition to draw on over here to help us do that. And maybe that's why we're not asking the key question about money. Why does there seem to be so little of it? Or why so little in Nether Wallop?

Once again, it isn't really about too little money. In parts of the economy it's absolutely sloshing around, but we have no tools to target our increases in money supply to one place rather than another. Complementary currencies might do exactly that – but they are a tool we have to use ourselves. And here you *can* see Populist roots in the UK: in the Rochdale pioneers and the libraries, in the Liberal tradition of self-help and the socialist tradition of co-operation, in housing co-ops and mutuals and time banks and the whole gamut of new economics.

So whether we keep the pound – but even more if we abolish it – we need the balancing mechanisms to help us see the world clearly, and that means a range of new kinds of money.

David Boyle is the author of *Funny Money, The Tyranny of Numbers, The Money Changers* and *Authenticity.* This chapter is taken from the New Economics Foundation's Alternative Mansion House Speech in May 2002.

Chapter 9

Subsidiarity

Bicycles are song
spheres within circles they
weave through shouting cars

The science of the local
John Ziman

Subsidiarity? What an ugly word! What does it mean? Was it an emanation from Brussels? Surely we can do without it, and just go local – globally if possible? No, we can't. Or only relatively local. Schumacher saw that, and came back to that same ugly word. So it is worth understanding.

Strangely, it came from the Catholic Church. The concept is as old as empire, but was not formulated until 1931. Pope Pius XII then propounded it as a moral principle: "It is an injustice and at the same time a grave evil and disturbance of right order to assign to a greater and higher association what lesser and subordinate organisations can do. For every social activity ought of its very nature to furnish help to the members of the body social and never destroy and absorb them."

The English word was coined as a literal rendering translation of a German paraphrase. For half a century, it remained pedantically theological. Then, in 1992, the states of the European Community found that it was precisely how they wanted to define their powers as nations in the Maastricht Treaty. So now it stands for a general principle of governance: *decisions should be taken at the lowest competent level in an organisational hierarchy.*

That may be what it is now called, but the subsidiarity principle is not news in domestic politics. Half the legal and legislative conflicts in the United States and other political federations are about 'states' rights'. Devolution from Westminster to Scotland and Wales is only the latest battlefield in the struggle for power between local, regional and national authorities in Britain. What is the minimum size for an effective police organisation, or a body responsible for schools, or for health services?

63

When we proclaim 'localism', we usually mean 'subsidiarity'. For example, we say that transport planning should be decided 'more locally' than in Whitehall. But just how 'local' should that be? It obviously depends on the mode of transport. Responsibility for footpaths can be devolved down to parish council level, but trunk highways may be beyond the competence even of county councils, so that's where 'regional assemblies' will be required. Political subsidiarity is one of the characteristic features of a free and open society[i]. It just means choosing for each function the minimum scale of operations for efficient democratic governance.

A multi-level economic system

But politics cannot be separated from economics. Our political system has many levels, from the town council right up to the Security Council of the United Nations. Surely this should be paralleled with a *multi-level economic system,* ruled by the same subsidiarity principle. The evils practised in the name of globalisation suggested to David Korten the necessity of creating "a multilevel system of institutions to reduce unnecessary interdependence and foster empowerment of the local"[ii]. Jeremy Brecher and Tim Costello go further: "The decaying nation-state economic system needs to evolve towards a *multilevel* one-world economy – local, state/provincial...etc."[iii]

More specifically, James Robertson[iv] has proposed a system of just six levels, corresponding to easily recognised geopolitical domains of increasing size. To give some idea of the arithmetic of subsidiarity, I have added rough estimates of the demographic and geographical scale factors for each of these levels (for a graphic representation of this see the chapter on trade).

Locality – for example a 'parish', 'village', 'neighbourhood', 'community', typically with a population of *a few thousand* living within *walking distance* of each other.
District – that is, a 'city', 'county', 'canton', 'department', or similar administrative unit, with a population in the order of *100,000* within a range of, say, *20 miles.*

Region – here this means a sub-national division of an existing sovereign state, such as a traditional 'province'; it might have a population of *several million* people and cover an area of about *100 miles* in radius.

Nation – a nation-state, as in the United Nations; these vary enormously in size, but might be supposed to be like the United Kingdom, with a population of *50 million* in a territory that is about *500 miles* across.

Continent – this category should really include large political groupings such as the EU, the Indian sub-continent, and China, each with a population in the order of *a billion* spread over distances of *several thousand miles.*

Globe – which for comparison has a population of six *billion* people distributed over a sphere where no two people are more than *12,000 miles* apart.

This scheme is, of course, very arbitrary, and shows up some of the inconsistencies in the world political system. Nevertheless, it is conveniently simple, even though, as Hazel Henderson points out, the 'Global System' actually includes a great variety of non-territorial entities, such as families, small and large businesses, NGOs and so on.[v]

Economic subsidiarity is thus emerging as one of the basic principles of new economics, in that it favours 'evolution from today's international economy to an ecologically sustainable, decentralizing, multi-level one-world economic system'.[vi] At present, nation states claim a paramount economic authority, which they are powerless to enforce, whilst global institutions such as the IMF exercise economic powers for which they have no popular authority.

But the debate on how economic decision-making powers should be distributed up and down this hierarchy has scarcely begun. No doubt the relevant bodies at each level should be able to impose *taxes* – like a Tobin tax on global financial flows – and spend the money thus raised (as now thoroughly established in the EU). But is there also a need, as argued by James Robertson[vii] and by Richard Douthwaite[viii], for a multi-level *currency* system to protect local economies against globalised money?

How big is a 'minimal' enterprise?

If economic subsidiarity is to be effective, it must involve more than taxes and interest rates: it must apply directly to 'the real economy' – that is, to industry, commerce, public utilities, transport systems, employment, and so on. The trouble is that this economy operates on a great range of organisational scales, ranging from family farm to international airline.

The present-day 'global' economy allows ownership and control of every type of enterprise to drift up to the multinational level, where it is notoriously unaccountable. This is absurd and inequitable for the production of bananas, but unavoidable in the air transport industry. In between these extremes, there are many activities, such as the manufacture of saucepans, or the running of railways, which would be quite uneconomic if undertaken 'locality' by 'locality', but do not really require a larger market than a 'region' or 'nation'.

Sooner or later, the desire to 'go more local' comes up against this basic fact of modern life. Sometimes this obstacle is tacitly ignored, and attention focussed on goods and services, such as 'food, furniture, construction, repair and maintenance services, as well as human services'[ix] that can indeed be provided at the 'locality' or 'district' level. But that still leaves a large fraction of what most people regard as essential to ordinary civilised life – including public services such as medical facilities – to the tender mercies of the predatory globalisers.

Unfortunately, it is not realistic to suppose that we could just live without these material benefits, or that the diverse problems of supplying them all equitably could be solved by one simple politico-economic formula. So the new economics must include a serious analysis of what might be called *industrial subsidiarity*, not just as a desirable principle but also as a practical possibility.

I haven't yet found any significant discussion of this issue. Perhaps this is because it doesn't have a general solution, but has to be considered industry by industry. But to get a handle on it, here is a straightforward practical question that might be asked in any sector of 'the real economy': *what is the size of the geo-demographic unit required to provide an adequate 'market' for a 'minimal productive enterprise' in that particular sector?*

Of course, this question is neither practical nor straightforward. All the terms in shriek quotes are up for grabs. But just suppose we plough ahead, and watch out for the torpedoes later. The answers might come out something like Table 1.

Table 1. Minimum size units for adequate "economies of scale"

Unit	District	Region	Nation	Continent	Globe
Size (miles)	20	100	500	2000	10,000
Population	100,000	2 million	50 million	1 billion	5 billion
Production	Food crops	Building materials	Clothes, textiles	Vehicles	Microchips
	Cash crops	Processed food	Small machines and components	Electronic systems	Pharmaceuticals
	Housing	Furniture	Electronic devices	Small aircraft	Large aircraft
		Hardware	Steel	Ships	
		Cash crop marketing	Oil, Gas, Coal		
			Civil engineering		
			Books, films		
			Bicycles		
Distribution	Fresh food	"Groceries"	Bulk commodities e.g. grain	Oil, gas	
Distribution (cont.)	Daily supplies	Clothes	Industrial machinery		
		Books			
		Cars			
		Household appliances			
		Cinema			
		Seeds			
Services	Schooling	Universities	Insurance	Aviation	
	GP medical	Hospitals	Railways	Shipping	
	House repair	Public Health	News media		
	Restaurants	Safety	Telecom		
	Hotels	'High Street' banking	Commercial banking		
	Waste recycling	Buses	Electricity		
		Theatre			
		Water			

What are the facts?

Now for the torpedoes. First of all, this whole table is guesswork. Nobody seems to know the actual facts. At one time economists did flirt with the notion that a firm might have an 'optimum' size, but this idea has largely been abandoned.[x] The only quantitative data that I have found so far date from 1969[xi] and show the percentage of the total UK market that could then be served by a 'minimum efficient sized' plant in various industries (see table 2).

By the standards of our present-day Europeanised and globalised economy, these look laughably small. In the 1970s, it might still have been reasonably economic for a small 'nation' to invest in a local oil refinery or a 'package plant' for ammonia production[xii]. In many industries nowadays, a single highly automated plant can easily supply the needs of a whole 'continent'[xiii].

Table 2 confirms the guesstimates of Table 1 that there must still be places for many effective enterprises at the 'district' and 'region' levels. But one must be careful not to misinterpret these data. A relatively small enterprise, such as a brewery, may well be able to operate quite efficiently with a million or so customers. That does not mean that its actual market should be restricted to a single 'region'. An even spread of plants over the land, each with a local monopoly, would no doubt be just the solution favoured by a national brewing cartel, or Stalinist government[xiv]. It is vital to have a genuine choice of products and services at any locality, in order to get the benefits of market competition. In this case enterprises should certainly be competing directly at the level of a 'nation', but not necessarily at 'continental' or 'global' level.

In these two tables, I have not tried to distinguish between the 'locality' and 'district' levels. In a standard text on economic geography[xv], I did find some old data about vegetable production around cities and about the distances people travel to shop for various types of goods, suggesting that these levels are not economically separable. Presumably much more about this sort of thing is now known, if only in the research departments of supermarket chains.

One can see that many sustainable activities such as solar energy and biomass technologies require short distances[xvi]. But it is probable that the economies of scale in general factors such as education, power, labour, and transportation combine to peak at an even larger unit size than a city of around 500,000 population – that is, at the 'region' level[xvii].

What is an enterprise?

The next torpedo is another question: what do we mean by an 'enterprise'? I suppose that it might be defined as an individual, private company, public corporation, not-for-profit organisation, governmental body and so on, devoted to performing a specific activity in the 'real economy'. For present purposes we limit this to any activity that can be regarded as 'self-contained', to the extent that it is managed as a single whole, and might figure as a distinct heading in a set of financial accounts.

Needless to say, this begs many questions about the extent to which any particular economic activity can be regarded as naturally self-contained. Apart from subsistence agriculture, hunting and fishing, all human activities are economically interdependent. Almost always one can produce a rationale for combining linked activities into a single enterprise. So this question used always to be answered maximally, as if it were quite natural for a single enterprise to cover a number of activities that could well be undertaken separately.

But the recent fashion for outsourcing and subcontracting challenges the doctrine of the optimal omnicompetence of the large firm. We are now into a much more subtle debate about the control that a large enterprise can exercise over its associates without actually owning them – for example, by long-term contracts, alliances, franchise agreements, brand names, and so on[xviii].

Table 2: Size of market required (in 1969) by a plant of 'minimum efficient size'.

Fraction of UK market	Industry
50 – 100%	Aircraft, Electronic data-processing equipment, Steel wide strip rolling, Electric motors, Motor cars, Refrigerators, Washing machines, Turbo generators
20 – 50%	Synthetic fibres (polymer production), Raw steel, Newspapers, Sulphuric acid, Ethylene, Synthetic detergents
10 – 20%	Synthetic fibres (yarn extrusion), Cement, Petroleum refining, Bicycles
1 – 10%	Beer, Warp knitting, Book printing, Cotton spinning and weaving, Bread, Plastic products, Large iron castings
< 1%	Bricks, Machine tools, Small iron castings, Shoes

Indeed, many multinational corporations are technically just holding companies for a hierarchy of operational 'subsidiaries', each registered as a separate firm – that is, as potentially a separate 'enterprise'. Other large organisations try to do much the same thing by establishing 'internal markets' between their various segments. Thus, nominal subsidiarity is already accepted as a management principle in the corporate world. So a simple defence against this torpedo is provided by commercial accountancy: any corporate activity that could in principle be treated – for tax purposes, for example – as the work of a 'subsidiary' firm, or of a subdivision operating in an 'internal market', can be considered a distinct 'enterprise'.

That is why, for example, we recognise that restaurants, hotels and cinemas are quite capable of operating individually, at the level of the 'district' or 'region', even though they may mostly belong to 'national', 'continental', or even 'global' chains.

Large is powerful

The third torpedo is more sophisticated. Economists agree that market forces produce efficient systems. The global economy is an open market. The current predominance of very large, complex enterprises is due to market forces. Therefore, they are all 'minimal productive enterprises'. Enough said. There is no point in considering a 'subsidiarised' system of much smaller enterprises since this would necessarily be much less efficient. Abandon ship, you new economists, and row for safety.

Well, in spite of all that is done on its authority, this argument is false at every point. Many economists don't agree that market outcomes are optimal. The present global economic system did not evolve in perfect 'market' conditions. Market forces do not curb the growth of un-productive monopolies. And so on.

Thus, economic subsidiarity is not a mirage. It is not at all irrational to suppose that many economic activities could be undertaken quite satisfactorily by much more devolved systems of quite small, relatively independent enterprises. In fact, such enterprises often survive for a long time in industries that are dominated by much larger ones[xix]. In effect, they constitute models for what might have been counted as 'minimal productive enterprises' under slightly less stringent economic conditions.

For example, many of the small shops that are put out of business by the arrival of a supermarket would probably have remained quite viable on a more level commercial playing field. They are victims of the 'market power' that a large firm can exercise to cut costs and prices in ways that have nothing to do with straightforward productive efficiency.

Again, many of the supposed 'economies of scale' are quite limited. For example, the increase in size of firms in many industries is not associated with increases in size of their productive plants or outlets and the gains from large-scale ordering for multi-plant firms are 'rare and insubstantial'[xx].

It is often asserted that direct access to research and development is a genuine economic advantage for large enterprises, but it could be that this benefit levels off well below the typical size of the largest firms[xxi]. Certainly, in the pharmaceutical industry, much of the work – and a lot of the risk – of drug discovery are undertaken by 'research boutiques' which sell patents to the global multinationals.

Where large is particularly powerful is in financial resources. A multi-plant firm, for example, can respond more flexibly to circumstances by transferring capital or operational balances from one part of the corporate system to another[xxii]. The fact that large enterprises also get bank credit on more favourable terms than smaller ones opens up the whole question whether it is feasible to apply the subsidiarity principle to financial institutions in general, over and above the issue of multi-level currency systems.

What is more, by accumulating profits and credit-worthiness, successful enterprises are enabled to make use of marginal facilities, take over less successful rivals, buy up suppliers, invest in 'upstream' and 'down-stream' enterprises and generally expand into areas of economic activity far beyond their core business. In many cases, the incentives to reduce trading risks by 'horizontal' proliferation and 'vertical' integration could be lessened by the use of financial and commodity hedging facilities[xxiii]. But the market power of a 'brand name' often relies on the creation of a 'global commodity chain' – that is, a network of labour and production processes whose end result is a finished commodity[xxiv] – where the intermediate enterprises are only nominally independent[xxv].

Facing up to the system

Nevertheless, in practice, one other factor is dominant – the *predatory* power of corporate capitalism. Enterprises grow excessively large mainly as a result of 'hostile' or 'defensive' mergers and takeovers even though these usually produce very limited cost savings[xxvi]. And the larger they get, the easier and more tempting it is for them to expand further, even when they are already much above the minimum size[xxvii] for reasonable economic efficiency. This is an intrinsic feature of 'free market competition', which manifests itself at every level of the 'global economy'.

This exploration of the principle of subsidiarity thus soon reaches a point where it has to face up to the nature of the system as a whole. Further analysis of the concept of a multi-level economy inevitably raises questions about how some of our present political and economic policies, practices and attitudes will have to be changed if we are ever to move in that direction. I would not hesitate to raise such questions, and to consider quite radical answers to them – but that would take us into another ball game, out of the area of this chapter.

John Ziman

i   Schumacher, E. F. (1973). *Small is Beautiful*. London, Blond & Biggs.: p.147; Henderson, H. (1999). *Beyond Globalization: Shaping a Sustainable Global Economy*. West Hartford CT, Kumarian Press. : p.51

ii   Korten, D. C. (1995). *When Corporations Rule the World*. London, Earthscan.: p.320

iii   Brecher, J. and T. Costello (1998). *Global Village or Global Pillage: Economic reconstruction from the bottom up*. Cambridge MA, South End Press.: p.174

iv   Robertson, J. (1998*). Transforming Economic Life: A Millennial Challenge*. Dartington, Green Books.:   p.25

v   Henderson, H. (1999). *Beyond Globalization: Shaping a Sustainable Global Economy*. West Hartford CT, Kumarian Press.: p.23

vi   Robertson, J. (1999). *The New Economics of Sustainable Development: A briefing for policy makers*. London, Kogan Paul.: p.6

vii Robertson, J. (1998). *Transforming Economic Life: A Millennial Challenge*. Dartington, Green Books.: pp.100-102

viii Douthwaite, R. (1999). *The Ecology of Money*. Dartington, Devon, Green Books.: p.72

ix   Sachs, W. (1999). *Planet Dialectics: Explorations in Environment and Development*. London, Zed Books.: p.206

x   Chapman, K. and D. Walker (!987). *Industrial Location: Principles and Policies*. Oxford, Basil Blackwell.: p.78

xi   Utton, M. A. (1982). *The political economy of big business*. Oxford, Martin Robertson.: p. 41, quoting, Pratten, 1971, *Economies of Scale in Manufacturing Industry* (Cambridge University Press) pp.269-277, CUP

xii   Schumacher, E. F. (1973). *Small is Beautiful.* London, Blond & Biggs.: p.156

xiii   Chapman, K. and D. Walker (!987). *Industrial Location: Principles and Policies.* Oxford, Basil Blackwell.: p.79

xiv   Chapman, K. and D. Walker (!987). *Industrial Location: Principles and Policies.* Oxford, Basil Blackwell.: p.63

xv   Lloyd, P. E. and P. Dicken (1972). *Location in Space: A theoretical approach to economic geography.* New York NY, Harper & Row.

xvi   Sachs, W. (1999). *Planet Dialectics: Explorations in Environment and Development.* London, Zed Books.: p.206

xvii Lloyd, P. E. and P. Dicken (1972). *Location in Space: A theoretical approach to economic geography.* New York NY, Harper & Row.: p.134

xviii Allen, J. (1995). Crossing borders: footloose multinationals. *A Shrinking World? Global Unevenness and Inequality.* J. Allen and C. Hamnet. Milton Keynes, The Open University: 56-102.: p.74; Castells, M. (2000). *The Rise of the Network Society.* Oxford, Blackwell: p. 168.

xix   Chapman, K. and D. Walker (!987). *Industrial Location: Principles and Policies.* Oxford, Basil Blackwell.: p. 78

xx   Utton, M. A. (1982). *The political economy of big business.* Oxford, Martin Robertson.: pp.44 – 46

xxi   Utton, M. A. (1982). *The political economy of big business.* Oxford, Martin Robertson.: p.48

xxii Chapman, K. and D. Walker (!987). *Industrial Location: Principles and Policies.* Oxford, Basil Blackwell.: p.117

xxiii Rubner, A. (1990). *The might of the Multinationals: the rise and fall of the corporate legend.* New York NY, Praeger.: p.239

xxiv Gereffi, G. and M. Korzeniewicz, Eds. (1994). *Commodity Chains and Global Capitalism.* Westport CT, Praeger.

xxv Klein, N. (2000). *No Logo.* London, Flamingo 2000.

xxvi Utton, M. A. (1982). *The political economy of big business.* Oxford, Martin Robertson.: p. 130

xxvii Penrose, E. (1995). *The Growth of the Firm.* Oxford, Oxford University Press.: p.261

Chapter 10

Time

A child, the clock hands
gave me orders, now its face
asks my opinion

Rebelling against the clock
Jay Griffith

"We do not recognise history, patriarchy, matriarchy...or lollipop men/ladies...Our currency is to be based on the quag barter system. We do not recognise the Gregorian calendar: this day shall be known as One..." Thus spoke British road protesters in a 1995 manifesto.

The clock and calendar have long been a locus for power struggles. Potentates, princes and priests, hypnotised by hopes of hegemony, have always stood on the borders of space and looked at time – for time is a kingdom, a power and a glory. When the ancient Chinese empire first colonised some new territory, the people of that region were said – in a sinister way – to have 'received the calendar'. Pol Pot declared 1975 Year Zero in Cambodia. Mayan priests in Central America gained their power over people through accurate knowledge of time. In 1370, Charles V of France gave an order that all clocks were to be set by the magnificent clock in his palace: he was the ruler of the land and now would be ruler of time.

But wherever there are clock rulers, there are clock rebels, and in the French Revolution Charles V's clock was severely damaged in an act of articulate vandalism. A new time-measurement was announced: 1792 became Year One.

The Benedictine monasteries began scheduling time and ringing bells through the night in the 6th century, controlling and ordering time according to Christian dictat. The Industrial Revolution created time-owners; the capitalist factory bosses, erecting clock-bound fences of work-time and the sense that employers owned the time of their employees, enslaving their time, enclosing it. Stealthily, nastily, one type of time has grown horribly dominant: Western, Christian, linear, abstract, clock-dominated, work-oriented, coercive, capitalist, masculine and anti-natural: *Hegemonic Time.* This time, and all the time-values which go with it, have been imposed on numerous cultures across the world – when missionaries arrived, the Algonquin people of North America called clock-time 'Captain Clock' because it seemed to command every act for the Christians.

There is revolt. The challenge to Hegemonic Time has come from the radiant variety of times understood by indigenous peoples, from self-conscious political protest, from children's dogged insistence on living in a stretchy eternity, from women's blood and from carnival.

Subversive and mischievous, carnival reverses the norms, overturns the usual hierarchies. Unlike Hegemonic Time, carnival is usually tied to nature's time. It is ahistoric, linked to cyclic, frequently seasonal events. Carnival transforms work-time to playtime, reverses the status quo. It is frequently earthy and sexual. The Puritans hated that, outlawing May Day and other festivals. Carnival also emphasises commonality: customs of common time celebrated by common people on common land. In Britain, a huge number of these customs disappeared as a result of enclosures, and when rights to common land were lost, so were the rites.

Carnival is vulgar: of the common people. And it is vulgar in another sense: drunken, licentious, loud and lewd – from May Day's Green Man's Horn, to apple-tree wassailing. Just as land was literally fenced off, so the spirit of carnival – broad, unfettered, unbounded exuberance – was metaphorically enclosed.

But carnival erupts, the deliberate use of costume amongst global justice protesters of today, for example, in Seattle, Gothenburg, London, Genoa, seriously playing out the politics of carnival – and indeed the politics of anti-enclosure.

Workers in Britain in the 1820s and 1830s smashed the clocks above the factory gates in protest at the theft of their time. Trade unions took on first the abuse of time, seeking shorter working hours. British workers staunchly persisted in honouring 'Saint Monday' and French workers 'Saint-Lundi' – in effect the patron saint of hangovers. Protest continued from the 1960s revolt against work, the refusal to wear watches, the slogan 'Work less, live more!' to today's 'Downshifters'.

Play, that subversive beastie, is anarchic, energetic and creative, is still hated by modern day Puritans of corporate capitalism. All over the world, colonisation included insistence on work time: Columbus, on first meeting the Tainos people of San Salvador, was convinced they should be 'made to work, sow and do all that is necessary and to adopt our ways...' The Innuit in Canada refer to themselves as 'rich in knowledge, meat and time'. Anthropologists have recently begun referring to hunting and gathering people as the 'original affluent society' in that the pleasures and necessities of life could be secured with the minimum of work.

One of the most tenacious conceptual threats to work, and to Captain Clock's Hegemonic Time, is childhood itself. Children have a delicious disrespect for worktime, punctuality, efficiency and for schooled uniform time. Their time is an eternal present. They live (given half a chance) pre-industrially, in tutti-frutti time, roundabout time, playtime. Staunch defenders of the ludic revolution, their hours are stretchy, ribboned, enchanted and wild: which is why adults want to tame their time so ferociously, making them clock-trained, teaching them time measurement as if they were concrete fact. The school clock is pointed to as the ultimate authority that even the head obeys.

The exterior public clock and calendar of Hegemonic Time is white, clean, regular, predictable, objective, linear, homogenous and male. I'm not. No woman is. It's in the blood, the inner, private, idiosyncratic, cyclical time: red, staining, alternating between ovulation and menstruation. Masculine society places a high value on people being the same over time, being reliable. But women (notoriously) are creatures of change.

I'd gleefully say *mea culpa* to the charge. When I'm ovulating, I'm not the same as when I'm pre-menstrual. At one pole I may well be co-operative, relaxed and nice. At the other, I will be intense, difficult, powerful and unpredictable. Probably. Menstruation gives women an experience of time that inherently subverts Hegemonic Time. Masculine society seeks to deny or penalize this time, to mock or scorn or (at best) ignore it. But this is where many women find their power, veering off at a subversive angle from the objective, public line of time. Menstrual absenteeism, deplored by many employers, is rightly relished by many women, for these days are quintessentially her own and do not belong to another.

Many cultures have cyclical ideas of time, essentially opposed to linear time – which, for all its dominance today, is an extremely recent concept. Among the Innuit of Baffin Island, the term *Uvatiarru* means both 'long ago in the past' and 'far ahead in the future.' In Hindu thought, time moves in the unimaginably long cycles of the Kalpas.

Opposition to Hegemonic Time is also found in moral values attributed to aspects of time: for example, speed. Although considered a virtue in itself by Westernised cultures, speed is immoral to many others. To the Kabyle people of Algeria, speed is considered both indecorous and demonically over-competitive: the Kabyle refer to the clock as the 'devil's mill'. In Brazil, the Xavante people have a ritual which involves two groups carrying two heavy logs, looking – to Western eyes – much like a race: but if one group falls behind, the other will slow down for them. Who 'won' is a baffling question to the Xavante, for this is not a race but an act of beauty.

Slowing down is catching on in the West as well. In France there is the anti-car newsletter Moins Vite!, in Italy a campaign for Slow Food, and in Austria an Association for the Deceleration of Time. Politically subversive singer Manu Chao's CD Esperanza notes: "*Este CD nacio de muchos trabajos, viajes, porros y encuentros. Nacio sin prisas…(porque las prisas matan…)*." 'This CD was born of much work, many journeys, spliffs and meetings. It was born without hurry, (because speed kills).'

Gutenberg's printing press printed calendars before bibles: Hegemonic Time was mass-produced to go global. In one of the most pernicious lies in history, the Christian calendar and the clock of capitalism insisted that they represented time itself. But the clock is not a synonym for time; it is an opposite of time. The Christian calendar (abstract, numerical and inherently political) has been used to deny the plurality of calendars across the world. Time itself, sensuous, poetic and diverse, is not found in it.

The leaders of the Zapatistas insisted their time was not the time of the Westernised Mexican government. The Zapatistas took their orders from the peasants, and this was a very slow and unscheduled process. "We use time, not the clock. That is what the government doesn't understand." Subcomandante Marcos, in March 2001 in Mexico City, spoke to thousands: "Tlahuica. We walk time… Zoque. We carry much time in our hands."

Among many peoples, timing involves spontaneity rather than scheduling, sensitivity to a quality of time that is unclockable. The San Bushmen of the Kalahari do not plan when to hunt, but rather 'wait for the moment to be lucky', reading and assessing animal patterns, looking for the 'right' time. Timing for many indigenous peoples is variable and indeterminate, optional and unpredictable. Time is a subtle element where creativity and improvisation, flexibility, fluidity and responsiveness can flourish.

What subverts the dead hand of the dominant clock? Life itself. The elastic, chancy, sensitive times chosen for hunting depend on living things: how the living moment smells. There is a 'biodiversity of time' imaged in cultures around the world, time as a lived process of nature. There is a scent calendar in the Andaman forests, star diaries for the Kiwi peoples of New Guinea and Aboriginal Australians who begin the cultivation season when the Pleiades appear. One indigenous group in Madagascar refers to a moment as 'in the frying of a locust'. The English language still remembers time intrinsically connected to nature, doing something in 'two shakes of a lamb's tail' or the (arbitrary and sadly obsolete) phrase 'pissing-while'.

Time in the past, too – 'dead and buried' under Western eyes – shimmers with life to many other cultures: the Australian Aboriginal dreamtime ancestors 'live' in spite of death: they disappeared, but did not die. Interestingly many areas rich in myth and indigenous history are shown to be places of high biodiversity; living history, life at its liveliest.

For time is not found in dead clocks and inert calendars, time is life itself: in ocean tides and the blood in the womb, in every self-respecting child, in the land itself, in every spirited protest for diversity and every refusal to let another enslave your time; in the effervescent gusto of carnival – life revelling in rebellion against the clock.

Jay Griffiths is the author of *Pip Pip: A sideways look at time.*

Chapter 11

Trade

Stories and spices
migrate like geese, while food
grows in a field nearby

A different economy
Andrew Simms

Free trade should be exactly that, free and not compulsory. Otherwise small fish can invite their own demise by having to swim into the mouths of bigger fish. Economic integration is not a panacea for global poverty and many countries that have opened themselves up to trade and capital flows have been rewarded with financial crises and disappointing performance. According to economist Dani Rodrik, turning away from world markets is surely not a good way to alleviate domestic poverty, but countries that have scored the most impressive gains are those that have developed their own version of the economic rulebook, while taking advantage of world markets at the same time.

Since the 1960s, almost every attempt by developing countries to engage with the global economy on terms that would help them develop, such as managing investment, regulating foreign multinationals and stabilising commodity prices, has been resisted and opposed. It is another echo of the 19th century when, according to Mike Davis, author of *Late Victorian Holocausts:* "From about 1780 or 1800 onward, every serious attempt by a non-Western society to move over into a fast lane of development or to regulate its terms of trade was met by a military as well as an economic response from London or a competing imperial capital."

The hypocrisy of this situation is laid bare by the historical facts on domestic market protection. Ha-Joon Chang produced the table below to show how both the two dominant economic powers of the last two centuries employed protectionist measures to establish their dominance before preaching free trade to the world. As John Kenneth Galbraith said: "Free trade was for the first arrival, where, as in Britain, it was indeed an attractive design for confining the later contenders to their earlier stages of development."

Average tariff rates on manufactured products in the early stages of development.						
Fraction of	*1820*	*1875*	*1913*	*1925*	*1931*	*1950*
UK	45-55	00	0	5	n.a.	23
USA	35-45	40 50	44	37	48	14

Rodrik also observes that: "US import tariffs during the latter half of the 19th century were higher than in all but a few developing countries today." To economic historians like Robert Heilbroner, the contradiction between historical reality and current mainstream economic rhetoric on the benefits from competitive international trade is not a surprise. He points out that for much of the last millennium, the "notion that a general struggle for gain might actually bind together a community would have been held as little short of madness".

Although trade relationships are as old as human civilization, most basic needs were met locally. Trade was for luxuries and special items not obtainable in the area. Where trade built the wealth of the first industrialised nations, it was often one-sided, exploitative, and to the cost of countries in Asia, Africa and Latin America. According to Davis, under the British in India: "Between 1875 and 1900, years that included the worst famines in Indian history, annual grain exports increased from three million to ten million tons – an amount equivalent to the annual nutrition of 25 million people." During 200 years of the British in India, Britain became a global economic superpower. India, on the other hand, saw no increase at all in the wealth of its people.

Even the conservative philosopher Karl Popper could see in the operation of free markets, pursued to their logical conclusion, a fundamental threat to an open global society. He talked of: "The paradox of economic freedom, which makes possible the unrestrained exploitation of the poor by the rich… results in the almost complete loss of economic freedom by the poor."

In today's global economy, incurable problems with depressed commodity prices, beggar-thy-neighbour South-South competition, environmental stress and the reluctance of rich countries to assist or open their markets to any significant degree, are still dismissed as minor irritations in the face of the long-term promised gains from liberalisation.

A dirty secret

> "For many Least Developed Countries, external trade and finance relationships are an integral part of the poverty trap."
> UNCTAD, The Least Developed Countries Report 2002, Escaping the Poverty Trap

Trade and development economists have disagreed with the dominant view of large, guaranteed benefits from trade liberalisation for many years. For example, the leading trade economist Paul Krugman wrote that there is a 'dirty little secret' in the analysis of international trade which hides the fact that the costs of protectionism "are not all that large", while the "empirical evidence" of great benefits from liberalisation "is at best fuzzy". Former World Bank chief economist and Nobel prize winner Joseph Stiglitz said that "it is not surprising that critics of liberalisation... raise cries of hypocrisy."[i]

There is a sense that, not only are rich countries pulling up the ladder, but that they are also mocking poor countries from their comfortable heights. According to Stiglitz, rich countries play down political problems faced by developing countries telling them to "face up to hard choices" – but then excuse their own trade barriers and agricultural subsidies by citing "political pressures". And it is not only political problems that poor countries face, including high unemployment and "weak or non-existent safety nets", but greater economic volatility, and the problem that "opening to trade in fact contributes to that volatility".[ii]

Rodrik observes that some of the best success stories from the majority world contradict the standard view:

> "Economic development often requires unconventional strategies that fit awkwardly with the ideology of free trade and free capital flows. South Korea and Taiwan made extensive use of import quotas, local-content requirements, patent infringements, and export subsidies – all of which are currently prohibited by the WTO. Both countries heavily regulated capital flows well into the 1990s."

China is also considered a great success story, yet ignored the Washington rule book. They refused to liberalise their trade and proceeded to integrate with the world economy on their own terms.

In spite of this, universal deregulation is still the mantra of mainstream economics. Behind the international trade system, overseen by the World Trade Organisation, remains a belief in the automatic benefits of liberalisation. Within this belief is a largely unrecognised dynamic – that we are moving towards a utopian endgame – a market free of 'red tape', of any rules constraining the private sector. The underlying theory is that progressive deregulation leads to progress. In reality, power, market failure and real world problems get in the way.

Economists like Herman Daly realise that the scale of growth beyond a certain point is "ushering in a new era of 'uneconomic growth' that impoverishes rather than enriches."[iii] Even the OECD has said that: "The negative scale effects of globalisation may turn out to be very large, effectively swamping any positive…effects."[iv] This observation is perhaps most clearly demonstrated in the case of the economic 'externality' of global warming.

Climate change and environmental limits to trade

Global warming demonstrates one way in which trade systems must work within the limits of environmental tolerance. It is described in full in the New Economics Foundation's report *Collision Course: Free trade's free ride on the global climate.*

International trade is particularly fossil fuel-dependent. And the world has committed to reducing the emissions from fossil fuels to prevent catastrophic global warming. But trade as a share of total world economic output has consistently grown, increasing our collective dependence on fossil fuels.

Conflicts between trade and the environment have risen to the top of the agenda over the past decade. Most discussion has focused not on the impacts of trade itself – through the transport of goods across national borders – but on the ways in which internationally traded goods are produced. The blind spot about freight has led to a double failure: first to appreciate the real impacts of rising freight movements, and second to introduce the necessary policies to shift freight onto a sustainable path.

The planes and ships used to move goods around the world are one of the fastest growing sources of the greenhouse gas emissions responsible for climate change. Since international air and marine freight fuels are not taxed or included in agreed targets to reduce greenhouse gas emissions, this worrying trend is likely to continue.

Each year, we ship, truck and fly ever more stuff across national borders. Standing now at an annual total of $7 trillion, flows of trade have expanded far faster than economic output. And freight activities have been growing in accordance with trade flows. The environmental impacts of this growth are mirrored in the growing share of transport related greenhouse gas emissions. A study in 1997 by the OECD and IEA estimated that the transport sector accounted for 20-25 per cent of carbon emissions from energy use for the year 1995. The average annual rate of growth of transport related carbon emissions – including international aviation bunker fuels – but excluding the marine equivalent – was 2.4 per cent between 1990 and 1995. Within the transport sector, freight transport – including marine, aviation, rail/inland water and heavy duty road vehicles – accounted for 55 per cent of carbon dioxide emissions in 1990.

General projections for growth in the transport of internationally traded goods indicates that in 2004, the year of the full implementation of the Uruguay Round commitments, there will be an increase by 70 per cent over 1992 levels. This is over 15 times greater than the 4.5 per cent directly attributable to the specific consequences of the Uruguay Round. If the projected 70 per cent increase in international freight transport was to materialise by 2004, the resulting increase in emissions would make a mockery of both the reduction targets set for industrialised countries, and the current exclusion of international freight from Kyoto controls. The carbon intensity of the path chosen by the Asian newly industrialised countries also suggests that new lessons will need to be learned before other majority world countries attempt to follow their example.

Other negative side effects

A study of the more immediate environmental impacts of trade liberalisation in developing and transition economies by the United Nations Environment Programme concluded that there were "serious negative environmental, and related social, impacts of expanded trade activity". These included:

- Land degradation,
- Water pollution,
- Biodiversity loss,
- Displacement of local, community-serving economic activity,
- Loss of common property rights in the shift to export led activity,

- Social instability resulting from structural economic changes,
- The failure and obstruction of policies designed to mitigate environmental impact.

Commodity prices

"If world commodity markets are left to the free play of market forces...the downward trend in real prices is likely to persist. Indeed... the downward trend might even be reinforced," Alfred Maizels, Oxford University

Falling commodity prices have led to severely declining terms of trade for many commodity producing countries. Consequently, large increases in export volume by commodity producers have not translated into commensurately greater export revenues. Primary commodities account for about half of the export revenues of developing countries and many developing countries rely heavily on one or two primary commodities for the bulk of their export earnings. As well as low prices, commodity-dependent countries also suffer from market volatility.

According to UNCTAD, compared with their value in 1980, the prices of coffee, tea and cocoa are now less than half. Agricultural raw materials have lost around a third of their value and other food products half. This means that while we enjoy cheap commodities a country like Ghana might increase cocoa production by 80 per cent over a ten-year period and only see its earning increase two per cent.

A decline in purchasing power of a country's exports means that they are unable to buy imported goods and services that are necessary for their sustenance, as well as generating income for the implementation of sustainable development programmes. It also prevents primary commodity producers from investing in safe and environmentally-sound methods of production.

It should be pointed out that the problem of collective adjustment – in which most developing countries followed IMF and World Bank advice to export their way to economic growth – has still not been addressed. Maybe it did not require the highest qualification in economics to predict that a group of countries increasing exports of like products, would help depress prices and leave those same countries running faster to stand still, or actually backsliding economically.

With the minor exception of price insurance schemes, and suggestions to destroy stockpiles resulting from over-production, there are no significant proposals left to deal with the scale of the problem of low commodity prices.

Intellectual property rights

> "Of all things, knowledge is that which should be most freely shared, because in sharing it is multiplied rather than divided." Former World Bank economist Herman Daly

All markets are framed by rules concerning property rights. Rules concerning property rights in international trade are written in such a way that tilts the field of play in favour of those countries that are already economically dominant.

Dwijen Rangnekar, from the School of Public Policy at University College London, has produced estimates indicating the scale of the imbalance. The top five beneficiaries from the TRIPS regime for the year 2000, in terms of receiving payment of 'technology fees' were, in order: United States, Germany, Japan, France, UK. The losers, in terms of making payments, included: Republic of Korea, China, Mexico, India and Brazil.

In another sphere, biotechnology companies claim that the engineering of plant genetic resources is needed to continue feeding the world and to help the poorest people combat nutritional disease. Actually, the patenting of seeds and plant varieties has merely expanded the market control of chemical, seed and biotechnology companies, without reducing starvation and malnutrition around the world. It is inhibiting research by increasing costs, limiting the availability of scientific knowledge, threatening the livelihoods of farmers, and prohibiting them from saving, exchanging and re-sowing seeds.

Though rarely understood as such, property rights are basically a right to exclude. Patenting genetic resources has been described as the act of "committing daylight robbery on the common property of humanity". An old UN study calculated that: "If a royalty was charged on biological diversity developed by local innovators in the South, the North would owe over US$300 million in unpaid royalties for farmers' crop seeds and over $5 billion in unpaid royalties for medicinal plants."[v] Today, given the increasing importance of intellectual property in the intangible asset base of companies, those figures would need to be revised upwards.

Some argue that the stronger the protection of property rights, the better it is for economic development, because they assume that it encourages the creation of wealth. Yet there are many examples in history in which the preservation of certain property rights has proved harmful for economic development, and where the violation of certain existing property rights – and the creation of new ones – was actually beneficial for economic development.

What property rights are protected, and under what conditions? Those are more important questions.[vi] Broad patents can have the perverse effect of stopping research and development. According to GRAIN, this has been documented in several sectors –for example, the oilseed industry – and 'blocking technology' has become a strategic value of patenting today.

This argues that rather than a one-size-fits-all Anglo-Saxon model of property rights, which is increasingly what is used, the international trading system needs an approach of locally-adapted regimes to fit the specific development needs of the country or region in question. A forthcoming paper from the New Economics Foundation – *Limits to Property* – will examine this question in more detail.

Uneven negotiating power

> *"People of the same trade seldom meet together… but the conversation ends up in a conspiracy against the public."*
> Adam Smith

> *"Firms are islands of central planning in a sea of market relationships."* Ronald Coase, Nobel laureate

Mistrust of the chief players in the global economy, transnational corporations (TNCs), is at the heart of the WTO's continuing crisis of legitimacy. Rubens Ricupero, the head of UNCTAD, argues that their impact "depends significantly on how well the host economy bargains," but that, "the capacity of developing host countries to negotiate with TNCs is often limited." And weak bargaining, he believes, "can result in an unequal distribution of benefits or abuse of market power by TNCs."[vii]

There is a deep irony in that the liberalisation mantra has been used to open up developing country economies to foreign multinationals. Daly quotes Chicago School economist and Nobel laureate Ronald Coase in a classic article on the Theory of the Firm, who noted that: "Firms are islands of central planning in a sea of market relationships."

Daly goes on to make a critique which is yet to be answered: "The islands of central planning become larger and larger relative to the remaining sea of market relationships as a result of merger. More and more resources are allocated by within-firm central planning, and less by between-firm market relationships. And this is hailed as a victory for markets! It is no such thing. It is a victory for corporations relative to national governments which are no longer strong enough to regulate corporate capital and maintain competitive markets in the public interest."

These dynamics might explain why the World Bank's head of trade policy once said: "WTO obligations reflect little concern for development and little appreciation of the capacities the least developed countries have... The context of the obligations imposed by the World Trade Organisation agreements... can be characterised as the advanced countries saying to the others: do it my way."

This is similar to Stiglitz's view that countries are finding themselves in situations where they are having policies imposed on them, not unlike the 19th century opium wars, when countries were told to open up their markets by the threat of military force – for the benefit of the dominant trading nation.

Yash Tandon, director of the International South Group Network (ISGN), has pointed out that no system of governance is legitimate or moral unless it has a judiciary that is independent of those who exercise power in the system. A judiciary should function on the principles of justice and fair play, and defend laws and rules of governance that are arrived at democratically and protect the weak against the strong. The WTO is supposed to operate by consensus where each member country has equal say. But the reality is very different, and key decisions are often made in small invitation-only meetings.

Litigation in the WTO system is also extremely expensive. This means that, whilst there are potentially hundreds of cases the South could bring to the WTO on non-implementation by the developed countries of their obligations to them, they cannot afford to use the disputes resolution system. There is also a further inequality built into disputes system because of the differing relative economic size of litigants. 'Punishment' in the system comes in the form of various permitted sanctions allowed to the successful litigant. But there will always, for example, be far more pressure for a small sub-Saharan country to comply in the face of a US complaint, than vice-a-versa. Small, economically weak countries will always have more to lose.

Where does trade go now?

There is no simple answer to the question of what we should do. This is simply because, in every different situation concerning different products and trade relationships, the recipe for mutual benefit and maximum environmental sustainability will be different. This argues for a much more flexible approach to the management of international trade, especially where the most economically weak countries are concerned. It argues, for example, that there should be both more special and more differential treatment, according to the development stage and social, political and environmental challenges faced by nations and communities.

We face increasing volatility in the global economy, environment and international political community. These volatilities affect the poorest people first and worst. The new question to ask of every policy is: will this increase or decrease the vulnerability of people and will it add to or take away from our collective security? And faced with those questions, trade deregulation has often been a disaster for the food security and economic prospects of the poorest people in developing countries.

Amidst the global economic chaos, we are witnessing the death of the assumption that all economic activity logically floats up to the global level. The future is more likely to be found by asking a different question: what is the right level at which to organise all the different aspects of our livelihoods – in the neighbourhood, or at the regional, national, bio-regional or global level?

The answers to these questions in terms of food production, manufacturing, retailing, travel and culture will describe a sustainable new world order. It will be more about localisation – in the broadest sense – than globalisation. It can also be described in terms of 'subsidiarity' or the 'proximity principle', or 'nearness'. It is a planned internationalism where we do globally what we must – in terms of rules and controls to distribute more equally the benefits of global economic activity (such as competition policy to regulate multinationals and mechanisms to restore and stabilise commodity prices), and locally what we are able, in terms of economic self-determination.

What sustainable trade might look like?

This exercise in thinking locally shows one model for economic organisation that would minimise unnecessary freight transport, both domestically and internationally. It operates on the economic maxim proposed by Schumacher that environmental and social benefits are maximised when the scale of economic operations are at the most local feasible level. He uses the same term used to describe the founding political principle behind the European Union – *subsidiarity*.

The table by John Ziman (see Chapter 10, p.67) sketches what a framework for sustainable trade might look like. The model assumes that lifestyles are not immediately changed, trading between units can take place through information networks, co-operatives and fair markets. It assumes also that low-cost capital is available for investment at all levels, and that there are mechanisms to stabilise agricultural prices.

The different zones are estimates for geo-demographic units that provide sufficient economies of scale for enterprises to succeed, but also give limits beyond which the costs of scale and economic integration can outweigh the benefits. The model implies a very different toolbox for the management of trade than the one currently available at the World Trade Organisation. The time is now right for a debate on what these policies should be.

Plugging the trade leak, internationally

Another model for trade in which poor and marginalised communities can better guarantee a good deal, is a global version of the 'plugging the leaks' innovation. Plugging the leaks addresses the problem that – in economies, small and large – most benefits leak out of poor areas to economically more advantaged areas and actors. This is then addressed by finding out where the leaks are, and plugging them.

Community development guru Jane Jacobs draws an analogy between the functioning of ecosystems and the way that economies work. She asks the question, 'Can the way fields and forests maximise their intakes and uses of sunlight teach us something about how economies expand wealth and jobs and can do this in environmentally beneficial ways?'

Such a simple question has profound implications for trade and development strategy. Jacobs criticises conventional approaches as embodying a 'thing theory' of development: 'The Thing Theory supposes that development is the result of possessing things such as factories, dams, schools, tractors... things subsumed under the category of infrastructure,' but these, 'don't mysteriously carry the process along with them. To suppose that things, per se, are sufficient to produce development creates false expectations and futilities. Worse it evades measures that might actually foster development.'

Jacobs says it is important to understand that economic life predates foreign-aid programmes and the investments of multinational corporations. These, she says, are 'relatively recent froth on economic life.'

The economy-ecology analogy sees exports as essentially 'discharges of economic energy' like clear felling and extracting timber from a forest. Successful regeneration, rather, is built upon maximum economic diversification. Whereas, at the heart of conventional macro-economic models there is a tendency towards specialisation based on the flawed assumptions of comparative advantage and international competitiveness.

'In an ecosystem, the essential contributions made within the (natural) conduit are created by diverse biological activities. In the teeming economy, the essential contributions made within the (socio-economic) conduit are created by diverse economic activities,' says Jacobs. In both systems, the diversity with which received energy in the form of either sunlight, foreign aid or other inputs and earnings are used, fragmented, and reused, determines the degree to which that incoming energy will leave evidence of its passage through the forest or community.

Measurement is needed to highlight potentially perverse effects whereby by aid and investment can actually lead to a drain on local resources, displace local enterprise or hamper reconstruction. Jacobs says, 'The practical link between economic development and economic expansion is economic diversity.'

A way to test the value of inputs to regenerating a community is to develop new ways of measuring how those inputs are taken up and used. The New Economics Foundation is creating ways to measure what it calls the *local multiplier effect*. In this analysis aid, export earnings or investment cannot be assumed to make a genuine contribution until they can be demonstrated to have expanded the basis for sustainable livelihoods, and not displaced other local activities.

Jacobs calls for a similar measure of the value of inputs to the local economy, which she describes as an *import stretching ratio*. This is a more general measure; arrived at by dividing the value of a settlement's production of goods and services by the value of the inputs it receives. Similar conclusions are being arrived at by new analysis of developing countries' experience of import substitution in the 1960's and 70's. Dismissed by official literature on its impact at the time, economists like Graham Dunkley say the approach was far more successful. Coupled today with a better understanding of past mistakes it suggests a wider range of strategies opening up for the majority world.

Plugging the leaks has been shown to work in local areas, but can attempts to create and keep wealth at the local level ever work as a model at the international level?

In Nilgiri, in India, they think so. A scheme called Just Change, that started as a campaign to win land rights for tribal people, has grown into a model of economic co-operation between marginalised communities in different continents. Though small now, it is a powerful example.

In order to win control of land, the community in Nilgiri had to have permanent occupancy. For this they needed to work the land and turned to growing the big local crop, tea. They started selling their tea in a fair trade scheme, partly in order to sidestep the tea barons who they suspected would take the biggest share of any profit. But then they saw a weakness in the project: they were charging a fair trade premium price to people who they considered as their friends. And they wanted to be able to sell fairly grown tea to deprived communities in the UK, at the lowest possible price, so that both communities of people could benefit.

They linked directly with community co-operatives in Britain. By 'internalising' the production chain within such groups, they have managed to prevent extra value being extracted by middle-men and other profit-hungry retail and production companies.

The founders of the scheme imagine that this model could be extended to other crops that have to be traded internationally, and that could one day even be traded between communities in their own currency, further preventing the leakage of wealth.

"It is an attempt to link producers, consumers and investors in a cooperative manner where ownership, risk and benefit is spread across the different players of the market chain," says Stan Thekaekara, originator of the project. "We think the time has come to take fair trade a step further".

Conclusion

> " I sympathise therefore, with those who would minimize,
> rather than those who would maximize, economic entangle-
> ment between nations. Ideas, knowledge, art, hospitality, trav-
> el—these are the things which should of their nature be inter-
> national. But let goods be homespun whenever it is reason-
> ably and conveniently possible; and, above all, let finance be
> primarily national."
> John Maynard Keynes, National Self-Sufficiency, 1933.

The problems of trade and scale can be summarised like this:

- International trade and financial liberalisation do not benefit developing countries in themselves. In fact, for many, these dynamics have been harmful.
- The freedom to integrate into the world economy on their own terms, pursuing a mix of policies specifically designed to meet their domestic development objectives, would benefit the poorest countries most. Such countries should be free to identify and engage in markets of a size and structure in which the distribution of benefits from economic activity will be in their favour.
- Given the historical record, industrialised countries are, and continue to be, deeply hypocritical in denying poor countries the same freedom to manoeuvre in terms of market protection that they themselves enjoyed in their early periods of development.
- Especially where barriers to success in global markets are significant, but also under other circumstances, localisation and targeted local development stand the best chance of bringing significant gains to some of the world's most economically marginalised people.
- International trade, like all aspects of the global economy, is a wholly owned subsidiary of the world's natural environment. Poor people suffer first and worst from environmental degradation, and for example from the rising disasters associated with global warming. For this reason trade, like all economic activity, must work within the limits of environmental tolerance and, in this case, the need to make radical reductions in carbon dioxide emissions.

International trade isn't working for the world's poorest people. The Doha round of trade talks shows no signs of radically changing that situation. Instead of concentrating on details to do with market access, many of us believe it is time for the government to ask more fundamental questions about the shape, equity and sustainability of international trade.

These questions begin with the most important one: whether any existing or proposed rules will increase or decrease the vulnerability of the people in need. We believe that managing risk and reducing vulnerability will be aided by a process of localisation.

In Johannesburg in August 2002, at the tenth anniversary of the Earth Summit, the New Economics Foundation organised a parallel conference attended by civil society groups from 43 countries, as part of the People's Earth Summit. The largest contingent of participants was from Africa, followed by a mixture of people and organisations from Europe to South Asia, North America, Latin America and a number of small island states.

Those present drafted a statement that said they were joined by a belief that international negotiations were "failing to provide real alternatives to the current unsustainable pattern of development". They went on to make a number of proposals that shared as a common theme: "The idea that we must move away from the current model of globalisation, dominated by the finance sector, and move towards a genuinely internationalist agenda."

Most important of all was what lay at the heart of that agenda. It was: "The rights of local communities to determine their economic path and protect their cultural and environmental heritage."

There followed a long list of measures designed to address the imbalances, systemic risks and increasing chaos of the global economy. It covered finance, trade and reform of monetary systems. It spoke of natural resource management, education and government accountability. A huge majority of the people present were from so-called 'developing countries'. Their voices are a cold shower for critics who find it comfortable to believe that anyone opposed to globalisation is already rich and simply 'anti-development'.

Here is an illustration from the experiences of the Bangladeshi development organisation UBINIG. It shows what localisation might mean in the context of a poor country in the Southern hemisphere. Farhad Mazhar promotes *Nayakrishi* which means 'new agriculture'. This is a form of ecological farming that attempts to undo the damage and declining returns of the so-called green revolution, whilst avoiding the economic traps and scientific uncertainty of GM crops.

Apart from the complexities of farming theory, Farhad makes a point of elegant common sense about trade and globalisation that displays a pragmatism and logical set of priorities typical of groups too often written-off as merely 'anti-globalisation'. Farhad says:

> "I'm not against the market, or even international trade. It's just that trade should be non-exploitative, and local needs should come first. Now we've found that Nayakrishi agriculture is more economically viable than conventional modern farming, many households are beginning to go into cash crops for the market too."

Ever more economists are also questioning economic integration as a panacea for global poverty. Nigel Poole of Imperial College supports the idea of 'selective market integration'. He says:

> "Targeting local development rather than global integration may... bring significant benefits to communities who's livelihoods can best be enhanced not by costly investments aimed at overcoming almost insurmountable geographical, economic and technological barriers to market access, but by investments in local assets and initiatives: a 'targeted local economy'."

Critics may say that by focusing on the 'local', people are turning their backs on the world and pulling up the ladder of economic development from poor countries. But that would be fundamentally to misunderstand both the proposals, and what is happening in the increasingly shaky global economy. Localisation is not an absolute, but a dynamic process. Instead of encouraging the economics of large and remote organisations, it promotes an economics of nearness and human-scale in which people have more control over their lives.

We believe this is part of a new economics capable of delivering human and environmental well-being internationally. It has common themes everywhere, but will look different wherever it grows. It will be a planned internationalism where local people are more in control.

Andrew Simms is policy director at the New Economics Foundation.

94

Selected references

i   Chang, H-J (2002) *Kicking Away the Ladder: Development Strategy in Historical Perspective*, London: Anthem Press

ii   Daly, H E, *Uneconomic Growth and Globalization in a Full World*, Natur und Kultur

iii   Genetic Resources Action International (GRAIN) (1998), 'Intellectual Property Rights and Biodiversity: The Economic Myths', *Global Trade and Biodiversity in Conflict*, No.3

iv   Jubilee Research (2001) *HIPC: Flogging a dead process.*

v   Kim, L (2002) 'Technology Transfer and Intellectual Property Rights: The Korean Experience', *Bridges*, November/December 2002.

vi   McMillan, M, Rodrik, D and Horn Welch, K (2002) *When Economic Reform Goes Wrong: Cashews in Mozambique.*

vii   Mulvany, P, Intermediate Technology Development Group (ITDG). Cited in 'Blueprints for patenting life' (17.11.00), *The Guardian.*

viii   New Economics Foundation (1999) *Behind our backs – public opinion, international trade the World Trade Organisation.*

ix   New Economics Foundation (2000) *Collision Course – free trade's free ride on the global climate.*

x   New Economics Foundation (2000) *'It's Democracy Stupid': The trouble with the global economy – the United Nations' role and democratic reform of the IMF, World Bank and the World Trade Organisation.*

xi   New Economics Foundation (2000) *Paradigm lost: Critical voices on globalization and the big hole in finances for development.*

xii   New Economics Foundation (2002) *Chasing Shadows: Re-imagining Finance for Development.*

xiii   New Economics Foundation (2002) *Ghost Town Britain: The threat from economic globalisation to livelihoods, liberty and local economic freedom.*

xiv   New Economics Foundation and Bangladesh Centre for Advanced Studies (2002) *The End of Development? Global Warming, Disasters, and the Great Reversal of Human Progress.*

xv   New Economics Foundation, BirdLife International and Oxfam (2002) *Measuring real progress: Headline indicators for a sustainable world*, RSPB.

xvi   Rangnekar, D (2003) *Intellectual Property Rights and Development: What has changed with the trade-related intellectual property rights (TRIPs) agreement?*, Seminar at the School of Public Policy, UCL, 24 February 2003.

xvii   Rodrik, D (2000) *Can Integration Into the World Economy Substitute for a Development Strategy?*, Note prepared for World Bank's ABCDE-Europe Conference in Paris, June 26-28, 2000.

xviii   Rodrik, D (2002) 'Forum Globalization for Whom? Time to change the rules – and focus on poor workers', *Harvard Magazine*, July-August 2002.

xix   Shiva, V (1997) *Basmati facts*, Research Foundation for Science,
       Technology and Ecology,
       http://www.vshiva.net/naturefacts/basfs.html .

xx   Tan, C (2002) *Tackling the Commodity Price Crisis Should Be WSSD's
       Priority*, TWN Briefings for WSSD No.14,
       http://www.twnside.org.sg/title/jb14.htm.

xxi   Tandon, Y, *WTO : What Strategies for the South?* http://www.south-
       centre.org/southletter/sl34/sl34-06.htm .

xxii   UN (1999) *The Realization of Economic, Social and Cultural Rights:
       Globalization and its impact on the full enjoyment of human rights*,
       Preliminary report submitted by J. Oloka-Onyango and Deepika
       Udagama, in accordance with Sub-Commission resolution 1999/8 /
       UN Document − E/CN.4/Sub.2/2000/13.

xxiii UNCTAD (2002) *The Least Developed Countries Report 2002,
       Escaping the Poverty Trap.*

xxiv   UNCTAD (various years) *Trade and Development Report.*

Chapter 12

Work

Work comes like winter
I shake the rain off at home
making my things wet

Keep it Small
Ed Mayo

In a modern network economy, work is better when it is small. This is not just the quality of work, but the quantity too. There is an inverse correlation between the size of firm and the number of jobs created in industrialised countries such as the USA and UK. In plain English, that means: across the economy as a whole, the largest firms have destroyed the most number of jobs and the smallest – the micro-enterprises, with no more than a handful of staff – have created the most.

But the primary benefit of human-scale work is the closer connection it can offer between personal choice and personal meaning. The idea of good work, of a meaningful livelihood within a framework of values, after all predates modern economists by many thousands of years. It is an ideal that in different forms most people have worked towards in most places for most of human history.

Much of the language economists use to talk about work today (employment, flexibility, contracting out, the labour markets, economically inactive...) is no more than bits of Lego. They can be assembled, fit together and sound good, but they don't capture the fundamentals of work. They don't answer the question 'why work?' At root, we need to understand work as about meeting human needs and creating human dignity.

Work is about more than employment. Good work is something of use or value to the person who does it, or for whom it is done. Many of the most important and fulfilling parts of our lives – such as caring, favours and parenting – fit within the description, but are not predominantly organised as employment. When people are motivated by a need, which inspires care – whether unpaid or paid – such as teaching or nursing, there can be a richness in the motivation, because it is needs-driven and it sustains people and society. It's about creating real wealth.

97

This is good work. Fritjof Capra explains: "We can't be empowered by work that destroys the environment around us or creates systems of inequality. No matter how our work is organised, it cannot fully empower us unless we believe in its purpose." Yet this is not how the culture and incentive system of employment operates:

- In paid work, people are often being rewarded in terms of money and status when they are behaving destructively.
- Those involved in this unpaid work, whether care, parenting or volunteering, suffer low status, poor conditions and often increasing stress and personal costs. The burden of this work continues to fall disproportionately on women, whether they are out of or in the labour market.
- The labour market itself continues to discriminate against the time, skills and competencies involved in different forms of unpaid work.
- The lack of pay matters. The financial opportunity costs of unpaid work generates tomorrow's social exclusion, as those involved lack the opportunity to build the assets and savings required for pensions or dealing with crises. This is a 'reproductive tax' on women and a considerable subsidy of effort and time by the poorer sections of society of benefit to the richer.

The Protestant work ethic has been used by politicians in more recent times to suggest that employment is a responsibility for all citizens. The 1649 Act in England offered vagrants a choice between work or whipping. It prescribed compulsory labour for all, including children, who had no means of maintenance. In support of this, the Puritans – as Margaret Thatcher was to do in the 1980s – quoted St Paul, that "if any would not work, neither should he eat".

In fact, St Paul, in his second letter to the Thessalonians, was saying nothing of the kind. He was urging members of the Thessalonian community that were "disorderly, work not at all but as busybodies... that with quietness they work and eat their own bread."

In modern times, it has been a hallmark of economic development that it brings into markets work that used to be unpaid. And it assigns a low status to work with no monetary return. Unpaid work is not simply a residual activity, it is systematically *disvalued* culturally and economically.

As a result, it is the labour market that exclusively defines how we organise and validate work within society – where those out of employment are dismissed as economically inactive. The results are all around us. We have two twin evils: mass unemployment on the one hand, and a large amount of socially-useful work in families and societies remaining undone on the other. It is hard to imagine a worse outcome.

Albert Camus wrote that "without work, all life goes rotten. But when work is soulless, life stifles and dies". Instead we need to distinguish good work from destructive activity, by looking not at monetary return but its contribution to meeting human needs.

Today's economy focuses on a cycle of 'work to consume'. It focuses on what we want and generates new things to want through advertising. It is less good at meeting what we need. In poorer countries these include food, health and shelter – all unmet needs for millions. In richer countries, the decline in many quality of life indicators suggests that other needs, such as dignity and self-actualisation, are not being met.

An example of good work in practice is time banking. This has been pioneered by Dr Edgar Cahn in the USA and my colleagues at the New Economics Foundation, in the UK. This is a system which credits the time people spend helping each other. While LETS (another local currency scheme) focus on exchange, time banking promotes gift relationships.

The 1,000 or so time banks running around the world exchange credits called anything from *time dollars* in the USA to *hureai kippu* ('ticket for caring relationship') in Japan. At the simplest, the idea uses a broker at the end of the phone, and allows people to earn time credits for each hour they help out in their local community – anything from peer tutoring by schoolchildren to telephone counselling by housebound older people.

The approach uses some of the principles of volunteering to put forgotten assets to use meeting the forgotten needs: but it goes further than that. Time banks create a reciprocal relationship between people and institutions, as well as between people and people, which ordinary volunteering finds it harder to achieve. It allows almost anybody in society, including the elderly and housebound, to give something back. It rebuilds a sense of trust. Time banks can:

- Measure and reward work in housing estates, schools, health centres – anywhere people's active participation is needed to succeed – to deliver the volunteers which make a difference.
- Link together a range of different local volunteer or other projects.

- Help people get access to learning or new skills without cash.
- Underpin a range of self-help training courses, or a network of phone counsellors, or volunteer health advisors – whatever is needed locally.
- Allow almost anybody in society, including the elderly and housebound, to make a contribution and feel needed.

In the Peckham HourBank, for example, this means that participants earn credits for doing jobs – an hour of your time entitles you to an hour of someone else's time. Credits are deposited centrally in a bank and withdrawn when the participants need help themselves. The group practice in Rushey Green is using time banking to galvanise patient self-help and support groups. In Watford, older people have been revitalising local services like waste recycling, local transport and homework clubs for children using time banking to unlock time, knowledge and expertise.

Time banking illustrates one element of good work, which is a recognition that unpaid work, as in most cultures over time, is based on reciprocity. While still little more than a pioneering set of pilots, they demonstrate that it is possible to innovate and develop new structured ways of developing self-esteem and personal fulfilment as well as access to goods, services and information.

Of course, real money too is needed to support good work. For some forms of unpaid work, such as caring and volunteering, it would be possible to extend the working families tax credit to cover a wider set of people. This is what Colin Williams and Jan Windebank of the University of Leeds describe as an 'active citizen credit'.

After all, if economists included the implicit value of childcare by parents or grandparents on benefit (by inputing an hourly rate of payment for those looking after children when considering their potential for other jobs), it would soon become apparent that it is crazy to penalise in relative terms those that do not choose employment.

I expect that we will see a host of creative, pragmatic initiatives that could be taken to orientate existing institutions to promote unpaid work in family and community. After a period of experimentation, we will know more of the scale of the challenge implicit in creating a new social settlement around good work across gender, age and class.

For example, business support programmes should better serve micro-enterprises. These link closely to family life. Two thirds of businesses in the UK have no employees. Of these, only around five percent are 'growth' firms typically targeted by governments for support. Even the renowned programme of long-term bank finance for the Mittelstand in Germany systematically excludes and marginalises micro-entrepreneurs.

For larger businesses, we are learning from a decade or more of mainstream 'work-life' business policies. There have been significant steps forward, including more flexible working hours, better parental rights for leave and the widening of best practice to include non-traditional families. At the same time, the greatest predictor of whether companies in the USA take up family-friendly policies, for example, remains whether they have recently downsized. Who wants to work for them?

We have a long way to go before business leaders and markets embrace the idea that there is more to life than busy-ness. In the meantime, at least for those with the choice, the number of people choosing human-scale patterns of work, will continue to grow.

Ed Mayo is the director of the National Consumer Council, and a former executive director of the New Economics Foundation.